GOD'S BIKER

SEAN STILLMAN

MOTORCYCLES & MISFITS

GOD'S BIKER

First published in Great Britain in 2018

Society for Promoting Christian Knowledge
36 Causton Street
London SW1P 4ST
www.spck.org.uk

The author and publisher have made every effort to ensure that the external website
and email addresses included in this book are correct and up to date at the time of
going to press. The author and publisher are not responsible for the content, quality
or continuing accessibility of the sites.

British Library Cataloguing-in-Publication Data
A catalogue record for this book is available from the British Library

ISBN 978–0–281–07942–1
eBook ISBN 978–0–281–07944–5

1 3 5 7 9 10 8 6 4 2

Typeset by Geethik, India
Printed in Great Britain by TJ International

eBook by Geethik, India

Produced on paper from sustainable forests

To Jayne and our four children whom we adore,
my parents and my sister, and to my parents-in-law;
who together as a family are a most precious gift to me
and have collectively taught me the most about faith,
hope and love,

Gyda'm holl gariad

Contents

Foreword

When people get 'converted', what do they get converted *to*? The way we often talk about it, it sounds as though it's basically a matter of adopting a new set of ideas, with perhaps a slightly unfocused confidence that Someone is going to make it all right for us. Of course, anyone who has found their life turned around because of Jesus knows how ludicrously thin that sort of description is. But it takes a book like this to show us just how much more there is to it.

This is a story of *continuing* conversion – a deepening awareness of who Jesus is (not only the source of eternal life but the man who uttered the Beatitudes and challenged everything we think we know about what is worthwhile in human life or achievement), and a deepening awareness of what, in the light of this, the Church has to be. Sean's journey with Jesus starts in childhood and has no single great turning point from darkness to light; but it's a story of always-expanding sensitivity to *where* Jesus is as well as *who* he is. And where he is is where he always is – at the heart of the most desolate human experience, alongside the most desolate human sisters and brothers.

In the years I have known Sean and the work of Zac's Place, I've watched this awareness come more and more fully to life. Sean has repeatedly turned away from simple models of Christian outreach and successful styles of innovative mission. He has sought out where Jesus is and gone there, with all the risks and the failures this entails – and there are hard-to-read pages here about these risks, and the literal, physical cost of being associated with a Church that so often and so publicly hurts and betrays people.

But faithfulness in and through the sense of spiritual exposure, even spiritual desertion at times – the Gethsemane moments – is what comes across here. Paul says to King Agrippa in the Acts of the Apostles, 'I was not disobedient to the heavenly vision': Sean has been obedient like that, to a vision that has unveiled Christ in the toughest and loneliest of places, in lives that seem as far as you can get from 'church' as we usually think of it.

Read the story about Jenny at the beginning of this book, and you will see something of this unveiling: no happy endings, only the clear showing forth of a Christ who will not go away, who does not ignore or condemn. That's the vision, taking flesh all over again in the back streets of Swansea.

Sean has shown me constantly what lies at the heart of the Christian community's life, and I am deeply moved and thankful to have the opportunity of saying thank you to him and to God for this. And I have to admit to an unregenerate delight that it is my beloved home town that has been home also to Sean and his work!

Rowan Williams
Master of Magdalene College, Cambridge

Introduction
The righteous brothers

As the congregation left the crematorium, the familiar frame of an ageing biker made his way towards me. A proud member of his motorcycle club for several decades, he had ridden the miles in all weathers, lived the lifestyle to the extreme and carried the scars to show for it. We had known each other for years, having first met in my early years of ministry. He thrust his right hand into mine, gripping it firmly as he embraced me with his other arm. His bloodshot eyes and long mane of grey hair framed a beaming smile as he said, 'That, brother, was a righteous service. Thank you.'

The emphasis on righteous was poignant, as we had often talked about this subject. He knew enough about my Christian faith to know that an authentic faith needs to be backed up with a righteous life, the kind that Christ spoke of. He took a similar attitude to his own life of commitment in his club, which he pursued with an almost religious zeal. He wasn't just a member, he wanted to be a righteous member. He lived and breathed the values of what it meant to be a patch-wearing biker, proudly displaying his colours on his back at every opportunity and doing whatever he had to do to defend the honour of everything they represented, and he was respected for it.

We had our differences of opinion in lifestyle choices, attitudes and concepts of God. We also had far more in common than the casual observer would assume from looking at our two very different club patches: his colours evoking striking imagery of death and Hades and my own centred around a blood-red cross with 'God's Squad' written around it. We shared a commitment to live what we believed wholeheartedly and without compromise. On occasions like this our worlds would embrace, and the purest form of what we both believed would come together. He was supporting a club brother in his time of need, because that's what a righteous club brother does. I was keeping it real, honest and compassionate as I led a community of people through their grief, because that's what a righteous minister, biker or not, endeavours to do in these circumstances.

For as long as I can remember I have lived amid an environment that advocates a righteous life. Doing the right thing. Virtuous, wise, just choices and the pursuit of good character are often unpopular, can be deemed boring and will almost certainly at some stage go against the grain of what the majority are thinking. At the time when Jesus hit the road with his mixed bag of oddball followers, a righteous life was advocated by many in the community, and was certainly something to aspire to, but Jesus' friends weren't at the top of that particular list.

Some of those considered to be the most righteous were the Pharisees, both in their own eyes and those of the wider religious community. On the surface, they knew it all: the Hebrew Scriptures, the prayers, the rituals and the rules. They loved the rules so much, they made hundreds more of their own to assist with keeping people in their place and their own position elevated. Their zeal for doing the right thing could not be faulted, and to many they were the real deal; they were the most righteous brothers in town.

As Jesus gathered his prospective followers around him on a hillside, it will have come as something of a surprise to them when he announced that they needed to surpass the righteousness of both the Pharisees and the experts in Scripture if they were to have any chance of grasping his message and the significance of the journey they were about to embark on. This will have seemed absurd; this motley crew of misfits and outcasts knew that their reputation didn't necessarily reflect a righteous life. Even if they thought they were making decent progress, society in general viewed many of them as no-hopers. What hope would they have of living up to Jesus' expectations of a righteous life, if it meant surpassing that of the elite Pharisees?

This is a question that has followed me my entire life. I have been surrounded by the Christian Scriptures, the church community and the rules that go with it. But if you dare to strip things back, what does a righteous life look like? Is it possible that we can become so preoccupied with getting the rules right that we can miss the point altogether and get it all wrong? Is it possible that we put on a solid performance to impress others but inside we know we are a walking bag of inconsistencies, contradictions and hypocrisies? Dare we consider that the righteous life may be found in some place other than on a religious pedestal?

This is my story; the milestones of my heart and the pit stops on a weary journey that searches for this righteous life. It's a story that includes the on-the-road mission endeavours of a bunch of Jesus-following motorcycling misfits as I established God's Squad Christian Motorcycle Club in Europe, brought from its native Australia. In doing so, we became entrenched in the lifestyle biker community and have become accepted and been tested in equal measure, as my parish became a network of smoky bars, clubhouses and festival stages.

This is also the story of the birth of a street-level mission church in Swansea, South Wales. Zac's Place is a small community of Jesus followers, where the most fragile of life's walking wounded try to work out their faith. Quite simply, they wouldn't fit anywhere else and possibly wouldn't be accepted as they are. It has become a place of glorious chaos and complicated beauty.

But the story runs deeper than starting new ventures. It's a story of unlikely encounters on the margins that have shaped this somewhat shy, nervous, preacher's kid. It's a story that has encouraged me to stick my head above the parapet and dare to believe that the righteous life in Christ is still subversive, transformational and not so far out of reach as we might think. It's a story that acknowledges that while so much of the bad stuff that goes on happens outside of our control, a lot of good stuff doesn't just happen by accident where there is a resolve to live differently.

There are moments of unlikely embrace along the way, opening up a new way of seeing, a new way of believing and, dare I say it, a new way of living. Somewhere within the dysfunction are the threads of faith, hope and love, but it doesn't always look that obvious. Before I go right back to the beginning, however, allow me to give you a glimpse inside our little corner of chaos where a light flickers in the darkness on a cold, wet, Swansea night.

1

The red door

In many ways it was like any Tuesday night at a Zac's Place Tribal Gathering. A motley collection of misfits sat around an array of old bar-room tables, which were adorned with open Bibles and mismatching mugs containing mediocre coffee. The gatherings were often unpredictable, such was the chaotic nature of many of the folk that were part of this earthiest of church communities.

I often describe these gatherings as a cocktail of an Alcoholics Anonymous meeting and a hospital casualty department. A mix of fragile lives, some with axes to grind, many with open wounds, seeking answers to seemingly impossible questions, made for anything but a predictable and cordial discussion. Most Tuesday nights the heavy steel red door, which goes straight out onto the street, would bang open at some point during the more structured part of the evening. It would often be a latecomer or someone who had just seen the light on and thought there might be a decent chance of a free meal, or a dry pair of socks. Interruptions were not only frequent, they were expected and accepted by a church community that was learning tolerance.

But this week was very different. The door banged open and in stumbled a friend of ours, a woman who looked considerably older than her 40 years. The punishing strain of years of alcohol and drug abuse had taken its toll on this beautiful woman, though at times her beauty still shone through from a compassionate heart. Just a few weeks previously, she had rummaged around in the black plastic bag that carried her few possessions to pull out a blanket to place on a chair to ease the comfort of another, who was recovering from recent surgery. But this tender act of kindness seemed a very long way off as she clattered through the doorway in a raging temper, hell bent on causing maximum disruption as quickly as possible. Verbally abusing just about everyone present, her drunken rant and intoxicated words brought complete chaos to our discussion on humility, which had been in full swing just moments before.

Usually I'm reasonably adept at steering a discussion, allowing as many people as possible to contribute. However, it's not a gift that came naturally, bearing in mind I spent most of my school years trying to avoid ever having to speak in front of the class. Open discussions rather than a performance-based sermon were the norm for our gatherings, but on this occasion I lost the ability to steer the discussion any further. It descended into a riot, our foul-mouthed friend sitting in the middle refusing to lower the volume or to show any kind of respect to either herself or anyone else in the room. It had the hallmarks of turning ugly, very quickly. Other regulars were getting restless, losing their temper or getting frustrated that the moment had been lost as once again this supposed sacred time had been interrupted.

As it turned out, our friend had good reason to be upset. She'd had a bad day (in fact she frequently had bad days). She had been sleeping rough for a number of years, and Welsh winters aren't kind to those who find themselves on the streets for sustained periods of time. Weeks and weeks of cold rain and biting wind ravage the body. The summers aren't that much better. However, there were some wonderful signs of hope that things could be turning around for her, thanks to the dedicated care of a support worker, while small community initiatives like ours, seeking to provide grassroots care and support, can become a lifeline. Occasionally, though not often, it gets taken for granted and abused, and this was one of those occasions. Having had a bad day in court, she had lost her mobile phone and been kicked out of a neighbouring church earlier in the day, and all this just added fuel to her fire. I also had fresh in my memory her animated face screaming at me just a few weeks before, 'How can God love me? Look at the state of me, I'm a bloody mess?' She wasn't particularly drunk then – that had been a relatively sober cry from deep within – but I knew how messy this could get, and we had a number of fragile and somewhat more timid people in our group that evening.

As everyone was getting more and more restless, I noticed one of our number, Glenn, disappear out of the room into the kitchen. Glenn and his family had relocated from Australia to voluntarily give of their time to assist us at Zac's Place, and he was on a steep learning curve. Suburban, middle-class, affluent Canberra was very different from Swansea city centre, which at the time was seeing some of the sharpest increases in street drug usage in the whole of Britain. As Glenn left the room I can remember thinking, 'Fair enough. I'm sure there will be a few more following shortly. I can't say I blame him.'

But what was about to unfold no one could have predicted. A few moments later, Glenn re-emerged from the kitchen carrying a bowl of water. He walked towards Jenny, our ranting, foul-mouthed friend. By now she was swaying precariously on an old wooden chapel chair, pushing its ancient legs to the point of collapse. It wouldn't have been unreasonable to consider just throwing the bowl of water over her, but this was never part of Glenn's plan – not least because that had recently happened to her. A local hair salon owner had tipped water over her first thing in the morning as she slept in their doorway. Regardless of the chaos, no one was going to be humiliated like that at Zac's Place. Glenn knelt on the grubby carpet at Jenny's feet, looked up at her and asked if he could bathe her feet.

This was no easy request by any means. Years of living on the streets in Swansea had exacted a huge price from Jenny's feet. They had apparently even featured on a TV documentary about trench foot, the condition that soldiers suffered with in the First World War, caused by spending months on end standing, walking, sleeping and fighting in wet boots. Socks don't just slide off when you have trench foot. You peel them off and it's not just the socks that come away. Rotting bits of flesh tear off. The pain can be excruciating and the stench is awful. Nevertheless, Glenn gently bathed Jenny's feet with his bare hands. As he did so, I have never seen someone's demeanour change so quickly. Within moments, her shoulders dropped, her cursing silenced; as she tipped her head back she started singing a very different song. Peace fell across the room, and she continued to hold everyone's attention as her somewhat fragile voice now began to sing the old Sunday school song, 'Yes, Jesus loves me, yes, Jesus loves me, yes, Jesus loves me, the Bible tells me so'. It was if all the anger, all the questions, all the pain had somehow begun to be addressed in that one simple, tender act of humility and service.

In my wisdom, I thought this was a good time to conclude the formal part of our gathering! I said a prayer of blessing and we resumed our usual custom of drinking coffee and eating exceptionally good homemade cake together. Amid the conversation around the tables that followed, one person was heard to say, 'We didn't get very far tonight, did we?' and another responded, 'Weren't you watching? I think we got to heaven!' When the evening gradually petered out Jenny departed with her arms around two friends, singing at the top of her voice, 'Yes, Jesus loves me', walking down the middle of the street. It had indeed been a special night.

Just over a week later, the local newspaper ran a headline story about a woman who had been found dead in Swansea city centre. This in itself wasn't an unusual story, as tragically at that period several people had died on the streets. This made the headlines because the woman had apparently been lying lifeless for a number of hours. People had assumed she was drunk or just sleeping, and been walking around her all afternoon. Some would have been filled with pity, some wouldn't have known what to do, while others, I am sure, skirted around this obstruction like she was rubbish on the footpath. But this was our Jenny and she had in fact accidentally overdosed. Only the day before she had been talking with her personal support worker, Jan, who was employed by the *Big Issue*, about getting off the streets and into accommodation. There were real signs of hope and a desire on her part to turn things around. And then this. All of us in her network of support were devastated.

Her death was treated as suspicious and therefore there was a lengthy process to follow before her body could be released for burial. One week on from her death, we organized a walk of remembrance, from Zac's Place to the place she died, a set of steps not far from the railway station. After our regular Thursday night soup kitchen, around 30 friends from the street community gathered; many of them had seen her as a 'den-mother' figure. Friends from her support network also came. We placed flowers, wrote tributes, said prayers, lit candles and placed bottles of her and their favourite drinks in memory of a precious friend.

I contacted Jenny's father to begin to make funeral arrangements. Once upon a time I would have run a mile from having to sit alongside a grieving family. But experiences change you, and by then I had come to realize the significant value in helping lead people through the deeply traumatic pain of saying goodbye. But I knew this meeting would not necessarily be straightforward. In fact, I expected it to be hugely complex. How wrong I was.

I met with a deeply gracious, caring man, who had been desperately wanting his little girl to come home. The never-ending Father's love was so evident in this dear man's broken heart. He showed me the long list of different mobile phone numbers his daughter had had over the years, and told me he had never given up hope. All he had wanted was a call to say,

'Dad, get me a cab, I want to come home.' At 40 years old, Jenny was still her daddy's little girl. We shared stories and began to make plans for paying a fitting tribute to his daughter and suitable ways for him and others to be aided in their grief. As I quite often hear when I sit with loved ones, there wasn't to be too much 'unnecessary religious stuff' and 'we're not that bothered about having hymns either'. But what this father did want was a song. He said: 'If it's possible, can we sing "Yes, Jesus loves me" at Jenny's funeral?' Naturally I was more than enthused and assumed he had heard the story of what had happened at the Tuesday night Bible study just a week previously. I assumed wrongly. He took a moment to gather his thoughts and proceeded to explain why he wanted us to sing that song. He fought back tears, then said, 'You see, that is the song I used to sing her to sleep every night when she was a little girl. That's why I want us to sing it.'

Even today, many years later, recalling this moment brings a tingle to my spine.

Amid all of Jenny's pain, all her heartache, her questions, her anger, her confusion, her betrayals; somewhere amid the madness and the chaos there was the faintest shred of faith that dared to allow a glimmer of hope in a very dark place. Somewhere in the middle of the muddle, there was a cry of the heart that dared to utter, 'God, if you are there – I'm not sure if you are, but if you are – give me the faith to have faith, to have faith that you might possibly still love me, despite everything.'

About 200 gathered at her funeral some weeks later. We listened to R.E.M.'s 'Everybody Hurts', which has a pleading, psalm-like lament quality, and we sang 'Yes, Jesus loves me'. Broken-hearted family, the street community, social workers, support workers, substance abuse counsellors, police officers, housing support staff, all wept together. The chaotic and the caring said goodbye and remembered a fragile soul who had been disregarded as a hopeless, homeless junkie. But we knew different. The song would have been one of the last songs she ever sang, as she had left us that night with her arms around two friends. I have no doubt that Jesus did love her, and that in that tender act of humility from Glenn, an ordinary guy who did know something of the love of Jesus, she experienced something tangible of God's love within her tormented soul, as the water gently soothed her sore and broken feet.

Every now and then something happens in your life that redefines how you see the world. This became one of those moments for our little chaotic community of faith. For Glenn it was life-changing. What if he hadn't acted on the prompt that came from deep within his soul to do something? Tragedy, questions and heartache often sit alongside mystery and inexplicable moments of revelation. This and other incidents like it have increasingly become part of my story as I have discovered, having spent my formative years growing up within the Church, that I was more likely to find God on the margins.

From the rushing of the wind and the beating of the rain on your face on a deserted night-time motorway to sheltering under plastic sheeting, sharing soup with a homeless friend. From the rolling hills of England and the valleys of Wales to the shadows and scars of Chernobyl and never-ending horizons of Australia. Sharing Eastern European hospitality of home-brew chilli vodka and the delights of indigenous insights. It's been one varied ride. It all seems a very long way from a small boy sitting in a pew watching his father preach. It was never supposed to turn out like this, as my mother's dented saucepan lids testified.

All I ever wanted to do was play drums in a rock-and-roll band.

2

Foundations

Despite the majority of my ministry over the last 25 years being in an urban environment, I am most at home in the open countryside. Away from the demands of people and out of range of a mobile phone signal, I retreat to the solitude of open spaces when responsibilities have bled me dry. Sanity is recovered in feeling the breeze, watching the graceful manoeuvres of red kites, smelling the newly ploughed earth or squelching through the woodland mulch. As I began the period of reflection prior to writing this book, I returned to my birthplace, a small village in rural Berkshire.

I retraced my childhood footsteps around the perimeter of patchwork fields, which now seemed considerably smaller than when I, my sister and our small group of friends would disappear all day in them. We'd often come home covered in mud, exhausted after a day of building ditch camps and unsuccessfully trying to dam up the stream. Hollowed-out trees we once played in had now rotted, but I returned to that same stream.

As the water gently passed and the snow fell, I recalled those memories. Twisting and turning its way through the fields, cutting along the valley, around the obstacles where the water rats would play, the stream was the constant in the seasonally changing landscape. Forty years ago all I knew of that stream was what I experienced within a stone's throw of our home. Later I learned where the source of the stream lies and how it weaves its way eventually into the River Kennet, then into the Thames and out into the sea many miles to the east. As I came to realize, long before I took my first breath and long after I take my last, the story is much broader than the fleeting moments of mystery we wrestle with and the beauty we marvel at.

The distant rumble of trucks moving along the M4 motorway and the regular flow of jets approaching London Heathrow airport 40 miles to the east had not stopped either. As a child I had no idea what regular friends both the M4, then newly built, and Heathrow would become, but there was always a sense of wonder as I looked up in the sky. Where was that plane going? You could set your watch by Concorde flying over each day just after midday. In fact, I harboured a serious desire to become an airline pilot. Journeys to Heathrow airport were quite frequent when I was a youngster. Dad was a regular traveller overseas for short-term mission trips, usually to the United States, so farewells and homecomings were commonplace. Even now, the slightest whiff of aviation fuel takes me right back to watching jumbos lethargically trundle down the runway and miraculously rise above the London skyline.

My father is a preacher and a very good one too, but as a child I found it difficult trying to explain to my friends what he did for a job. Driving a truck for the gravel company would have been so much easier to talk about! From when he came to faith in Christ as a teenager, my dad knew a clear sense of a calling into the ministry. First and foremost, he has the gift of an evangelist, and he is most animated when speaking of the Lord. I use the word 'evangelist' cautiously, not because I doubt my father's commitment but because of its modern-day connotations. Unfortunately, the original essence of its definition – a bringer of good news – has been somewhat diminished by a brand of TV preacher that seems to be more like bad news, where too many of them have been found to be greedy and manipulative. Similarly with the expression 'born again'. Although it is imagery Jesus used only once, when talking to a religious teacher called Nicodemus, it has almost become the single definition ascribed to a Christian. 'Are you one of those born agains?' people will question nervously. When I ask the enquirer to give me their understanding of what a 'born again Christian' is, sadly a definition often comes forth that is based on either evidence or perceived impression of a self-indulgent, shallow, performance-based religion with a manipulative sales pitch leading the charge. This has coloured the impression of a skewed version of Christianity that is closer to big business and market-driven goals than to the gospel of Jesus of Nazareth.

That isn't the kind of Christian faith I grew up with. I have been privileged to see – modelled by both my parents – a lifetime of sincere, quiet devotion, living simply and faithfully serving God. My father's primary focus for ministry (over 50 years at the time of writing) has been to minister to men in prison. Long before there were dedicated mission organizations working in the prisons of England, he stumbled upon an opportunity.

It was the mid-1960s and a less regulated era when the entire prison population was permitted to gather in the chapel for dedicated worship services, and also for entertainment. My father had been cutting his teeth preaching in local rural chapels and was instrumental in setting up an outreach to young people. These efforts were based for a time at a building due for demolition where Reading's inner distribution road now sits. Here, at a coffee bar called Nu Kreetcha, local bands performed and the young preacher would give a short message explaining the heart of Christ's message and the transformation that Christ brings. He hadn't been formally trained for this. It seemed that God had set him aside, gifted him, and he was obedient to that call, a call that the wider church community recognized.

Out of the blue he received a phone call from Oxford prison. They had heard he had a film projector and a collection of various films that he had been showing at church-based youth events. The prison had a couple of hundred inmates expecting to watch a film on Sunday afternoon and they'd been let down for some reason. Could he go in and show a film? Any film would do. The young preacher was up for it, knowing full well that the only films he had at his disposal were gospel-oriented. He agreed to go and show the film, but only if the prison would allow him to offer a few words of reflection to the men gathered there after the film had finished, and make some simple literature items available for the men to take away and read if they wished. The authorities agreed and the young evangelist walked into a prison for the first time and took an opportunity to share his faith with the entire population in one evening.

This struck a chord with him. Here was, bizarrely, an open door to minister among a community of men who would generally never go anywhere near a chapel or church if they were out of prison. He not only saw the possibility, he had compassion and a desire to meet their spiritual needs. He also had the ability to communicate simply and effectively. Neither was the realization lost on him that in one evening he was able to present a case for the Christian faith among more non-believing men than all his pastor colleagues in the whole of the Thames Valley in a month of Sundays. From that point on, prison was his primary area of ministry, and he terminated a promising career in industrial chemistry to carry that forward.

One of the things I have treasured most throughout my life is his and my mother's commitment to this cause and calling. It took a long time as a child for it to dawn on me exactly what he was doing and where he was going. He'd be visiting Dartmoor, Winchester, Strangeways, Wormwood Scrubs, Pentonville, Long Lartin, Huntercombe, Bristol, Cardiff, Broadmoor and a host of other prisons, covering in excess of 30,000 miles a year. These were among the names I saw on his study calendar, week in week out. Occasionally I'd hear stories from the wings about men he'd been visiting for ten or more years, or how the 'screws' had been particularly cranky. Sometimes we'd have a phone call at home from someone in prison; I fondly remember him exchanging books with Ronnie Kray on a Broadmoor visit. He was, on a regular basis, voluntarily locked up with men segregated from the rest of society, in a confined space, because he believed that this was where God had called him to be. He's a great Bible teacher and communicator and could easily have pastored any church he wanted, but he hasn't allowed the lure of a more glamorous or high-profile ministry to steal away the call that still burns in his heart. Even now, in his seventies, he continues to minister regularly in a number of English and Welsh prisons and has contributed significantly in developing numerous initiatives in prisons to assist inmates pastorally and with their long-term rehabilitation.

The only potential diversion from this was a 12-month foray in the early 1970s to the USA, when we moved as a family to Virginia, on the east coast. Here Dad took up the invitation to minister at a Southern Baptist Church. He continued to minister in prisons there also, while preaching at a series of travelling mission meetings and other events. My sister and I did a year of elementary school there and had picked up a broad southern drawl by the time we came back to Berkshire, much to the amusement of our friends. Living near the huge US naval base in Norfolk, Virginia, and the air force base in Langley meant that there were often open days to go to where we could look at jets and walk around ships. For an eight-year-old boy, this was heaven! I even managed to score a handshake with President Ford at the commissioning of the aircraft carrier USS *Nimitz*, after he heard my English accent.

I call it a potential diversion because I certainly think that if we had stayed there my journey could have panned out very differently. I probably would have rebelled against just about everything presented by a right-of-centre, highly militarized, American nationalist brand of Christianity that was still living under the shadows of Vietnam. It was a long way from the Jesus movement that was happening on the west coast. But good memories remain: of generous hospitality, hay rides, river baptisms, the aroma of azaleas, Chesapeake Bay, and for the only time in my life being the best in class at soccer!

During our childhood, Dad was often on the road. Mum took her responsibility very seriously in seeing that my sister, Kerry, and I had a clear understanding of the Christian faith from a young age, but she never rammed it down our throats. It was very fitting, then, that it was through discussion primarily with my mother that I felt able to make my own decision to follow Christ. Her quiet, diligent witness and commitment to prayer continue to be evidence of a faithful life lived. Over the years, though, she has borne the brunt in the worry department. Her husband is ministering in prison on a regular basis with known violent offenders, I'm doing what I do and Kerry has committed her life to ministry in a remote mission hospital and tribal community in sub-Saharan Africa.

In 2004, my mother's worry proved to be well founded, as we received a call from one of Kerry's colleagues. She was experiencing gradual paralysis, which had started from the feet was slowly moving up her body. Her medical training was enough for her to know that she could be in a life-threatening situation if the paralysis continued upwards to her vital organs. I spoke with the mission agency, who recommended she be immediately medically evacuated, probably south to Johannesburg. I engaged in these calls while pacing outside our local hospital where my heavily pregnant wife was sitting at the bedside of our eight-year-old son who had been admitted with a severe asthma attack.

In a frightening series of events and within just 20 hours, my sister was in the Royal Berkshire hospital in Reading, instead of Johannesburg, having been evacuated from her remote mission station just in time. There was vital equipment on the German air ambulance that wasn't available in their isolated community and it had kept her alive. The sight of her lying on the trolley, with the orange dust of the sub-Saharan village still on her feet, was deeply concerning to say the least. What followed was a roller-coaster few weeks of subdued lights, chilling beeps of intensive care monitoring equipment, ventilators, and a long, long period of rehabilitation; she had to teach herself to eat, talk and walk again. She has her own story to tell and it's not my place to tell it here, but my little sister was a huge hero to me even before this. A hero she remains, as she returned to the dust and the community where God has led her as soon as she was medically fit enough, 15 months later.

My mother's journey was quite different from my father's. Born to a young unmarried Irish girl in Reading, whose own mother was from Galway, she grew up initially in the Catholic faith. She was adopted at seven years of age by the couple who had provided both her and her natural mother with a secure space to live, in a small terraced house opposite the cattle market in Reading town centre. Mum's natural mother opted to make a new start; my mum had new parents and a move to a brand-new council house. This adoption was a huge adjustment for her and it has taken most of her life to process it fully. She was given a beautiful, loving environment in which to grow up, and my grandparents continued to exhibit throughout their lives the kind of compassion they showed that young girl all those years previously, living in that same council house for the remainder of their lives.

My grandfather (my mother's adoptive father) was a Welshman, from Barry Island, who married a Reading girl just a few days before the D-Day landings began. Nan was a kind-hearted lady whose tiny kitchen was always stacked high with trays of eggs, waiting to be used in endless batches of cakes given as gifts for family, neighbours and whoever was passing through. The lounge was a similar hive of activity as she skilfully operated a huge industrial sewing machine. Its colossal noise would shake the whole house, only punctuated by the horse-racing commentary on the TV, and the pile of skirts would gradually grow on the carpet in front of the machine. It was a hard-working household and a deeply caring home.

In the last days of my grandfather's life I made several trips from Swansea to Reading to spend time with him in hospital. I remember it being bitterly cold with snow and ice thick on the ground as Christmas approached. He was becoming frailer by the hour, but still shared old stories, recalling memories never mentioned before from his experiences during the Bluecoat and Market Garden operations in the Second World War. He told how just weeks after their marriage his bride was given notification that he was missing in action in Belgium just prior to the liberation of Antwerp. To think that their marriage union – of well over six decades – was thought to have been brought to an abrupt end within weeks of the wedding is just staggering when I consider his impact on our family.

This small-framed, hard-working man was becoming more and more breathless. As I listened, he gave fading but firm instructions on where I could find his unwritten Christmas card at home for my grandmother. We brought it in for him, and as always, true to form, he had a pen handy. Men of his generation never seemed to be without a biro in their top pocket. I held the card up for him, and with the tiny amount of strength he had left, his glasses precariously perched on his nose, he managed to make the nib connect with the surface of the card. In the frailest of pen strokes, his normally precise, neat writing now spidery but his words as sincere and eloquent as ever, he declared his undying love to his bride of 65 years, thanking her, and their God, for a lifetime of companionship.

We sealed the envelope with tears and embraced. Knowing this would be our last meeting, I kissed him on the forehead, telling him that there were things I carried in my heart that only he had taught me. This small man, who always wore a tie, who was never without a packet of mints in his pocket, who had worked six days a week in the railway sheds, who took care of his own family and others, possessed very little material wealth yet seemed the richest man on earth, was a giant in my eyes. Even in his final breaths, he was still teaching me.

My father's parents were an odd pair to look at. My nan was a Londoner, well under five feet tall but full of East End cockney confidence. Whether it was cooking up pig's trotters on the hob or organizing the Women's Institute, she knew what needed to be done and she got on with it. She had been a housemaid at Shaw House in Newbury when she met my grandfather, who lived locally. He was a colossal six feet plus of army boxer. My memories are distant as I see him in his garden hunched over a shovel, turning the soil that surrounded their tiny cottage. His skirmishes in northern France were with the British Expeditionary Force, and had concluded dramatically as he was evacuated on the last ship from the French coast in 1940. Writing now in an age of instant global communication is a far cry from his method of communication to let his sweetheart know that he was home safe from Hitler's advances. As my granddad's train sped through Mortimer station he threw a scribbled note out of the window, hoping the station master would find it on the platform and pass it on. He did.

My life has been shaped by a depth of faith and love in a remarkably simple way, by a family that is in many ways very ordinary, but has at times been seen as different. As a child, though, you don't want to be different, you just want to be like everyone else.

I hated school. It seemed like ten years of nervous stomach ache and fear. Two main contributing factors were my diminutive stature, being around a couple of years behind in growth compared to most of my peers, and having a father who was a preacher. Not that I ever resented his choice of profession. I have always been immensely proud and thankful to God for my parents and the example they have shown me. But it certainly gave ammunition for those who saw me as an easy target. People handle these things in different ways and I have never enjoyed confrontation. My significant shyness, lack of confidence and crippling nervousness throughout school meant that many straightforward interactions outside of a few trusted friends were fraught with huge insecurity.

My first days at secondary school epitomized everything I came to dislike about the whole experience. I had gradually built up courage over the six-week summer holidays, but then the dreaded day came. I went believing all the stories about things that happen to new kids, but it wasn't the other children I needed to worry about. On the first day, the entire school gathered in the main hall, with the senior pupils standing at the back, and everyone assembled gradually decreasing in height to the front row – where I nervously stood adjacent to many I didn't know, all of them still taller than me. The deputy head teacher proceeded to give a 'welcome to the school' speech.

An abrupt, cold character at the best of times, mid-sentence and partway through his introduction he stopped and looked directly at me. His permanently furrowed brow and expressionless, tanned face inspected me. My significant lack of height had caught his attention. In his heartless, patronizing manner, he asked me where I was from. I muttered nervously I was from the village, down the bottom of the hill. He then went on to suggest, to the hilarity of what seemed like all 800 pupils, that my legs must have got worn down walking up the hill. On the day I had been dreading I had been humiliated in front of the whole school by a bully of a stranger who was demanding our respect. Part of me died that day, particularly the part that might foster any desire for academic achievement. Some of the deepest scars any of us will carry will not be flesh wounds but the scars of humiliation at the hands of a cowardly bully. I wasn't confident or brave enough to rebel, so I kept my head down, got my schooling done and looked forward to my earliest date of release.

My confidence was on the floor most of the time. I'd hide behind classmates in lessons, hoping I wouldn't have to read out loud. This would frequently backfire as teachers seemed to find great amusement in getting the shy preacher's son to read out loud, especially the erotic bits of the literature course. Or the maths teacher who got his entertainment from giving me adult film titles as we acted charades. Why we did charades in maths I'll never know. Not only was my physical growth delayed, my character was being stunted. I loved sport, but I couldn't compete as I was smaller than everyone else. I was the boy on the rugby pitch hanging on to someone's shirt, being towed along, flying in the wind like a wind sock, with no chance of getting a tackle in. In the big scheme of things these are minor issues compared with the deeply traumatic experiences some pupils have endured in the education system in decades past. But this stuff eats away at you; it messes with your head and at such a formative age it can shape what happens in the rest of your life. It tells you that you don't fit, you don't belong, you are there to be humiliated.

As I have matured – and eventually I did grow – I have gained the stability to channel my questions and anger in a manner that isn't either completely self-destructive or vindictive. Thankfully for me, I had the parents I have, a stable home environment and the security of some good friends, both within the church community and in school. But it's a very fine line; none of us may be that far away from becoming a dysfunctional wreck. We continue to be shaped by the environment we are nurtured in, for good and ill.

Growing up as a preacher's son and within a church environment were always going to leave a mark. At the time, there's no way of guessing which direction it's all going to go. I've seen much heartache and breakdown within the families of those in ministry. There's a peculiar kind of pressure that a pastor's family can be under. For us it was a little different as Dad was on the road speaking and involved in missions rather than being a local church priest. It's easy for people looking on to assume that the minister and his family somehow ought to have superpowers and children with self-cleaning teeth. It really becomes a problem when the minister and the congregation both start believing that.

Over the years I have pastored and supported ministerial colleagues who have found themselves thinking they are leading a double life. In public, everything looks great. In reality, the minister's spouse is on antidepressants, the daughter has no respect for them and their son is an amphetamine addict. In this perfect performance brand of church life that gets peddled around there is no room for a warts-and-all faith. The mess and the truth of ordinary human relationships affect us all. Sadly, the Church can be a very unforgiving environment for those who dare to live with transparency and honesty. It will come as no surprise that the conditioning of my character within the context of church was nowhere near ordinary. It's rather ironic that some of my earliest memories of church are encased in a sensual capsule of stale cigarette smoke and beer.

When I was born my parents were part of the Anglican Church, though my mother was of Irish Catholic descent. By the time I was to be blessed as an infant, they chose to dedicate me in the Elim Pentecostal Church as an alternative to the Anglican christening. Baptism was to be reserved for a time when I could make my own decision, and they committed to raise me in the ways of Christ. The beer and cigarette smoke came from none of those three denominations, however. As Dad's on-the-road ministry took him away from home a lot, particularly on Sundays, it was important that we as a family had a local church connection within the village my parents had settled in, particularly as mum didn't drive at the time. This came in the form of a small independent Evangelical church that met in the home of Alan and Marjorie McCarley. They were a remarkable couple, incredibly industrious and deeply committed to providing a children's Sunday school for the village. While there was a small gathering of adults in their home on a Sunday evening, a much larger number of children gathered to attend a Sunday school in the afternoon. The McCarleys' humble two-bedroomed home was never big enough for those gatherings, although I have fond memories of what seemed like a dozen of us piling into Alan's old black Ford Consul on a regular basis! Instead, the Sunday school moved around various locations – closed-up chapels, schools, and in this particular period of time the bar of the local working men's club.

By far and away the biggest collection of buildings in our village was the Royal Ordinance Factory, which at the time was not shown on Ordnance Survey maps for fear the Russians might find it. I grew up a few miles from Aldermaston, where the government's atomic weapons and research agency was based. These two sites, along with Greenham Common, have been the focus over decades for many demonstrations, marches and protests from peace activists. Aldermaston was where the research happened, and the factory in our village, Burghfield, was where the weapons were assembled. Occasionally you could hear convoys of trucks moving equipment out in the small hours of the morning. This factory was a big employer locally; in fact, my grandfather on my father's side was a fireman there, and other family members and school friends worked and did apprenticeships at Aldermaston. The peace marches that came and went when I was young seemed to pass me by. Maybe it was because so many in the village relied on the place for work, and our church experience at the time didn't make much room for 'tree-hugging hippies' campaigning for nuclear disarmament. The gospel for me was about salvation and repentance with a righteousness that had little emphasis on speaking out on matters of injustice, poverty or war, but was strong on the proclamation of the gospel.

So it was in the social club bar of a missile warhead assembly plant that I used to go to Sunday school. The pungent smell of the previous night's cigarettes and pipe tobacco lingered in the air and in the fabric of the soft furnishings. The floor was sticky with beer and the drip trays still full, as this motley collection of children were rallied into singing gospel songs, playing games and listening to stories. It was an important formative time, when the stories of Jesus really began to take shape for me. No one got paid to do anything in this church environment, it was just a mixed group of volunteers pulling together their limited resources in whatever place they could find to teach and demonstrate the love of Christ.

As we got older we chose to get involved at a larger Baptist Church community in the west of Reading. Again, this proved to be an important move and it became somewhere I was able to gain some confidence, and build friendships with others my age who also shared faith in Christ. It was no surprise that not long after starting attending there, my sister and I chose to be baptized. It was Easter Sunday and I was 12 years old. Even at that young age, and though I knew little of life and faith, I was prepared to make a commitment to follow Christ, despite the obvious ribbing I got from schoolmates. The friends I made in the church youth group proved to be a life-saver, giving me additional determination to stand up and be counted, and I benefited from regular peer-led Bible teaching.

Today I still delight in opportunities to speak with groups of young people who are growing up within the church environment. The Church is not always very good at nurturing and developing the faith of those who are growing up among us. We feel threatened by their questions, their motives and their rebellion, when that is exactly the time we should be nurturing, guiding and mentoring them. More often than not our own insecurities do not allow them the freedom to fly. This causes communication to break down, and our determination to strengthen the boundaries that define who's 'in' and who's 'out' takes precedence over seeing a life of faith form and mature.

The day of my final O-level exam, 24 June 1983, couldn't come quickly enough. School had continued to be a chore and an awkward experience, and I cycled home in celebration, enjoying the sunshine, feeling the breeze and looking forward, with a certain amount of fear, to discovering where this river would run.

3

The masks

———◦———

I cycled home in the sunshine knowing the awkward struggle of school was done. Of course, launching myself into the big wide world brought its own worries. I was still lacking in confidence, barely five feet tall, and due to start an apprenticeship as a draftsman in civil engineering. This wasn't a bad choice, but it wasn't my first; it was my third. While I'd done well in technical drawing at school, and it was the only subject I ever got a prize for, so it was an obvious choice, in reality I'd wanted to be either a pilot or a drummer, or both. Neither was viable.

One of my favourite songwriters, Bruce Springsteen, once recalled in an interview that the first time he looked in the mirror and liked the look of what he saw was when he hung a guitar around his neck. I could relate to that, although for me it wasn't guitars. I had begun to build my identity around drums and motorcycles. I'd loved the idea of playing drums ever since I first sat behind a kit at the age of eight when we lived in Virginia. We'd been visiting a family in Baltimore and I'd generously been allowed down to the basement of their home to play the drum kit. That was it, I was sold! The noise, and the potential for releasing a mix of emotion and physical exertion made it an experience that sat well with me. Unfortunately it was another eight years before I had the opportunity to acquire my own complete kit. Within weeks of starting work I arranged a loan from my grandfather of £400 to purchase a five-piece Tama kit on sale at Anderton's music store in Reading. I turned the volume up to 11 on my second-hand hi-fidelity record player and mercilessly thrashed my way through an assorted record collection of rock, metal and blues songs – drumming along with varying degrees of success, but mostly failure. The neighbours were in the main long-suffering, thankfully.

At the same time I got into motorcycles. My head was first turned by bikes when I was a small child riding in the back of the family Vauxhall Viva. While accompanying Dad to a preaching engagement on a Sunday morning somewhere in the Midlands, a pack of bikes came thundering past us with an almighty roar; about a dozen riders each wearing identical patches on their backs, their colours proudly displaying their tribal identity. They made an impression that would linger in my subconscious for years.

During my teenage years, a guy would pull up to church on Sunday evenings on his bike. He seemed pretty cool, had a few stories and wasn't like everyone else in church. He was going through a rough time, his marriage had disintegrated and he had decided to check out the church once again. I was then 14 or 15, and he became the big brother I didn't have. I started hanging out with Bob. I'd ride on the pillion seat, though as I look back today with a little more insight I'm not entirely sure how straight his head was. But hey, I went to a few places, met different people and saw things a son of a preacher wouldn't have got to see otherwise. Most of all, it gave me the opportunity to learn to ride a bike.

With a bike, when you make a mistake it usually hurts, a lot. You therefore learn pretty quickly. I was very fortunate the first time I dumped the clutch on Bob's old Honda. I pretended I could start it and Bob called my bluff. He said, 'If you can start it, I'll let you ride it.' The pressure was on! I managed to kick-start it, I engaged what I thought might be first gear, dumped the clutch and launched myself down the church driveway towards the main road, barely in control. Once the front wheel hit the ground again I just pulled, pressed, twisted and trod on every available option. The bike came to an abrupt halt, the engine revs hit the sky and with a jolt forward I stalled. I had successfully managed to travel 30 yards and not broken anything, either the bike or me. I was hooked; my passion for riding motorcycles had begun.

Bob patiently taught me how to ride safely and ensured that by my seventeenth birthday I was on the road with learner plates. For my 25-mile commute to the drawing office my bicycle was replaced with my mean machine of a Honda CB100N. I'd borrowed the money to buy my drums, but I'd saved up to buy the bike; it cost £170 along with extra for a lid, jacket, gloves and boots. Bob had drilled into me the importance of wearing good gear on the bike. 'You'll need a second skin one day,' he repeated. He dragged the back of my hand down a brick wall and took a few layers of skin off my knuckles just to illustrate the point that it'll hurt a lot more, bouncing down the road at 30, 40 or more miles per hour.

My initial euphoria at being on the road was short-lived, as one day the cam chain chewed its way through the engine casing and spewed oil everywhere. I found myself walking home, pushing the bike, bitterly disappointed, but soon learned that this was an occupational hazard of riding old bikes and not maintaining them properly. Long cold hours spent in a mate's garage, and bus rides to the breaker's yard to buy a second-hand engine, were all part of the experience of getting on the road. That, and riding. And did I ride – even on learner plates I was everywhere. I'd be back and forth to west London to see the likes of Gary Moore and Michael Schenker play live at the Hammersmith Odeon. On the cold November day I passed my test, in Henley-on-Thames where the waiting list was shorter than in Reading, I must have ridden a 100-mile detour home. And all the while Bob was with me. He had got me into bikes and, as it turns out, I think I helped to reintroduce him to his Christian faith.

When I wasn't out on the bike I'd be playing the drums, and it didn't take me long to get involved in bands. What I lacked in ability I made up for in determination. I was still very much a novice, self-taught with a dubious sense of timing and little technical ability. Very little changed over the following years, I might add; I just became more aware what my inabilities were, kept it simple and worked hard. I would practise for maybe 10 to 15 hours a week, and eventually got myself a tutor as well. Throughout my later teenage years my whole life became obsessed with playing drums. I landed on my feet for my first proper set of gigs; at the age of 17 and still a novice, I found myself playing venues for the over 21s and alongside others far more established in their craft. I loved the whole experience. It petrified me and electrified me at the same time. Within the first few songs of each gig I would be dripping with sweat, while the crack of my Ludwig 402 snare drum between my ears and the punch in the guts of the bass drum going through a huge sound rig fed an appetite to find out who I wanted to be.

I was still short and insecure, but I was now beginning to like the person I was seeing in the mirror. Gigs came and went along with several bands over the following years. Rehearsal rooms, persistent practice, endless loading and unloading gear, became routine. My bikes got bigger and I travelled further afield. The masks I acquired – hiding behind a drum kit on a stage and on the road a pair of sunglasses and a bandana across my face – became my identity. I was no longer Sean the shrimp. I was Sean the drummer, I was Sean the biker. But I was trying to work out who I really was and what I was going to do with my life.

My faith matured; I asked questions, particularly around the nature of what the Church appeared to be. Jesus was definitely cool, and so were some of his followers, but the Church, which I was beginning to distance myself from, seemed remote. My main connection with fellow Christians came through a network of Christian bikers. I joined the newly formed Reading branch of the Christian Motorcyclists Association (CMA). It turned out to be an important step at that stage; it gave me some travelling companions who were seriously into their bikes but who also carried a genuine, sincere faith in Christ, which they wanted to share with others.

There had been a lot of talk about a deeper faith experience among some of my peers at church. This became an unsettling time, as discussions were taking place from which I felt excluded. This was possibly not deliberate, but I certainly felt there wasn't anything I was expected to contribute and it seemed that there was a two-tier faith thing going on. There were those who had had this deeper experience and those who hadn't. Apparently, I didn't qualify.

From what I could work out, most of this experience involved congregations being whooped up into a frenzy and secret discussions concluding in the laying on of hands in prayer. I was made to feel an outsider, and to be honest the whole thing seemed a bit suspect. Without wanting to throw the infant cries for acceptance out with the dirtied bathwater, on reflection I think I was right to be cautious. What followed was to some a rolling wave of revival, but to others it was a mere emotional frenzy that did little except promote a feelings-based faith for congregations looking for entertainment. When the church community around me was flinging its arms in the air in jubilation, I was hovering by the back door, ready to walk. I began to think that genuine seekers of truth, who had once had a desire to follow Jesus, were buying into an experience and not a desire for ongoing transformation. This troubled me.

This search for a spiritual/emotional church experience was becoming an addiction in itself to some of those around me. The fact that someone can be reduced to tears when the worship band strikes up a song in a minor key should come as no surprise. Songs in a minor key do that. You may or may not pass it off as the work of the Spirit of God, but don't assume that's the case just because it makes you feel emotional. Lots of things in this world make us feel emotional; we are emotional beings. I was starting to ask some serious questions of the Church in general when the so-called charismatic movement, heavily influenced by the North American church, began to have a big influence on the Christian circles I was moving in.

So I was feeling isolated and almost second class in terms of my faith experience, but I continued to enjoy band gigs and many miles on the road with my new biker mates. Some of them have remained my closest friends on the planet, well over three decades on. Great friendships are formed on the road. I learned this early on with riding bikes; it's one of motorcycling's attractions.

A chemistry forms between you. It can be freezing cold, with rain beating against your face at 70 miles per hour and the bike only firing on one cylinder, but you've got your mate alongside you. As you pull in at the petrol station, sopping wet, fingers numb, you still find strength within you to keep going; someone will even crack a joke maybe, as pale-faced motorists look on as if you are mad. This kind of relationship doesn't exist in many other circles.

Even within churches, our structures and gatherings make it difficult for relationships to develop. Newer expressions of church remain very performance-oriented, with an 'us and them' barrier, those at the front doing their thing with the rest watching. The healthiest relationships are those forged when people work together in acts of service to others, or go through adversity together, not through pumped-up self-gratification experiences. It's like the difference between a repeating pattern of short-term relationships that make you feel good for a moment and a sustained lifelong commitment; while you don't get a permanent emotional high, you do feel something of substance that truly feeds your soul with a sense of wonder and completeness.

I didn't give up church completely, but I had some serious questions that nobody else seemed to be asking. Everyone seemed to have plenty of opinions, but no answers to my questions. More importantly, my questioning of what the Church was all about coincided with a genuine hunger within me to absorb deep within my soul what it was to be a follower of Jesus. I began to read the Bible more – not out of a sense of duty but because I was hungry to be fed.

I became fascinated with the stories of Jesus on the road. In one of my Bibles the words of Jesus are written in red, and these words became a magnet. My faith was becoming less about being the son of a preacher, and less about what people at church might think about me. It was becoming more about this person Jesus and whether there really was a bigger picture; and if there was, how was I to live in response to it? I began to understand why my parents' daily routine began with time put aside to read the Bible and pray. I had always wanted to do the right thing, but now this became my own much deeper search and experience. There was a hunger to be doing what God wanted, where and with whom he wanted. I didn't know it at the time, but I was looking for a righteous life, one that utterly surpassed that of a polished performance.

I was still very conscious of the fact that I never had a dramatic, 'blood and thunder' conversion experience. The church where I spent my teenage years, which eventually commissioned me into mission work, had very close connections with a wonderful Christian-based drug rehabilitation centre. Yeldall Manor was started in the early 1970s by Bill and Joanie Yoder. They were a beautiful couple who were close friends of my parents and tremendous examples of Christ's love and devotion to the marginalized.

In the early days of that ministry, Dad would sometimes be out late at night with Bill, searching for one of their house guests who had absconded back to London; they would find him among his old mates and dealers. I was aware from a very young age that some of these guys were around a lot for a while, then disappeared. They often relapsed; some overdosed and died. Although protected from the messiness of the chaotic world of addiction, I was well aware of its catastrophic effects. The legacy of the Yoders' foundational work continues at Yeldall, a community of transformation and hope.

As a result of our church's connection with the Manor, residents would often be asked to give their testimony, to tell how they came to faith in Christ. Of course, virtually all their stories involved prison, violence and a host of drama leading up to their conversion. In comparison, mine seemed rather dull and boring. It was actually many years before I had the confidence to tell my story. It took a long time for me to realize that my story was 'my' story. It's the only one I have. I discovered this on a visit to another drug rehab unit, when I was developing more confidence, and sharing my story there gave me great encouragement.

As I rattled off all the things I hadn't felt the need to do, and spoke of making a commitment when I was very young to follow Christ and keeping God at his word and sticking with it, the lads at the rehab were blown away. The residents responded by saying that they wished they hadn't had to go down the roads they did before they found faith in Christ. Since then, I have taken every opportunity to encourage young Christians in our churches to be confident of their story. When it comes to journeying with Christ, no stories are more spectacular than others. They are all a work of God's grace deep within our soul, carrying a depth and resonance with the ability to transform how we think and live.

As I continued to feel increasingly comfortable in my own skin, although wearing the masks of biker and drummer, I received a very sharp reminder of my own priorities. On a damp January night I was riding my brand-new Kawasaki into central Reading to see my drum tutor. The bike was three months old and was and remains my one and only new motorcycle. As I turned into my tutor's street, the scenario unfolded that every biker is constantly aware of.

People in cars don't see you. They don't see you primarily because they are not looking for you. Their attention is elsewhere; talking to passengers, adjusting the radio, lighting a cigarette or nowadays talking on the phone or messing with a sat nav. A blue Austin Allegro came directly out of a side street, failing to stop at the junction, and travelled across my path. I had just enough time to alter my direction to avoid t-boning the front wheel arch at 90 degrees and instead collided head on at an angle of 45 degrees. The first thing the blissfully un-aware driver, who was looking the other way, knew about it was the huge bang of the impact and the windscreen being smashed by my legs as I somersaulted over the roof of the car.

The crunching, smashing and scraping cacophony of noise, subsiding into silence, is a haunting experience. As you are flung through the air in what feels like slow motion, bouncing and sliding to rest in a crumpled heap, amid the smell of spilt fuel, your senses are both finely tuned and strangely muffled. Those few fleeting seconds seem to take for ever; then as you land with an almighty bang you enter real time again, emerging in a vague and disorienting fog. There's a mixture of relief that you're still in one piece – you hope, because you can't be sure – and then shock as the pain kicks in. You lie there with everything spinning around you and a mix of anger and disbelief, not coherent enough to communicate anything, but fully aware of the warm mushy feelings to your limbs, hidden beneath your clothing. My brand-new bike was utterly trashed, beyond repair, and I had come to rest in the gutter, 20 yards from my drum tutor's front door, surrounded by a sea of blurry faces, almost cartoon-like around me, frantically trying to communicate with me.

My mate Bob's advice paid off big time. The sole of my left boot was ripped off by the lip of the car bonnet and my left knee left a perfect imprint in the bike's fuel tank which sat atop a now twisted frame. I was very fortunate, partly down to my decent riding kit and partly down to God's mercy. That particular type of accident usually causes much more serious injuries than I received. I was back on a bike in a couple of months, although the insurance company only paid out enough for me to buy a second-hand model of the same machine. The driver was fined for dangerous driving and after several years I was compensated for the injuries. These days, if you see me struggling with my knees, that is partly the reason why.

If you ride a motorcycle, a certain amount of tar surfing is inevitable. Because mistakes hurt, you do learn not to make them. But you can never second-guess what another motorist is going to do, and the road surface itself can be a hazard: a diesel spill will make it like ice, there may be debris to avoid or wet leaves in autumn. With experience, you learn to ride defensively and I tend to treat every vehicle around me as a loaded gun aimed in my direction. I've covered approaching half a million miles by motorcycle, but that doesn't make me immune. Part of the exhilaration of motorcycles is the edginess of it, but like everyone on the road, or those who sail, climb or fly, you always have to be respectful and alert to the things that aren't in your control as well as the things that are.

This accident was a timely reminder for me of what was important. In retrospect, it probably started me questioning my priorities. I had already completed my engineering apprenticeship and chosen to leave the company to do short-term contract work, so that I could concentrate on my drumming aspirations. Where did my faith fit in? Did it mean enough to challenge my ambitions? The irony of my new bike being smashed up on the doorstep of my drum tutor's house wasn't lost on me. The two things I was pinning my very identity on were called into question for the first time.

These questions hovered as I exited my teenage years, weighing up what I wanted out of life. What did I want to do, and did I dare consider including God in the conversation? If I had given up on motorcycles then, after my first major smash, I would have missed out on some wonderful experiences and lifelong friendships forged on the road. Similarly with church, I realize as I reflect on my questions at the time – if I had walked away I would never have met a wealth of beautiful creative people and a community of mentors and friends who have had a profound impact on me ever since. There were always reasons to close the door on it, but I didn't; or rather, I couldn't.

I was beginning to feed more on the Scriptures and I began asking what my response to Christ's teaching would look like for me. I was ready to work hard and make sacrifices in pursuit of musical ambitions, and free enough of other responsibilities to give it a go, but did I dare ask the question of God: is this the wisest path to take? My prayers had an increasing sense of urgency and depth about them; I genuinely wanted to know. Christ's challenge of 'seeking first his kingdom and his right-eousness' came as a renewed choice with a fresh responsibility to act. I was aware of a shift from acknowledging a firm belief in Christ and his teaching to actually doing something about it, rather than paying lip-service and riding on the coat-tails of a preacher father.

The band I was in during this period was based in Buckinghamshire. I made the midweek ride out there in all weathers for our regular rehearsals at a studio in Great Missenden. I'd leave the bike at the guitarist's house and travel with the lads, using the studio's drums for rehearsal rather than carting mine around in between gigs. We had played together for about a year and the little profit we made from gigs we put into studio time to record demos and send cassette tapes around our contacts. We had gathered some momentum and were making headway. The other four lads had grown up with each other, but they accepted me from the start, right from my audition in a rehearsal room in Reading. We were a bunch of 19-year-olds who were committed to the cause, worked hard and were receiving some good reviews.

One of our regular venues was the Coal Hole pub on the Strand in central London. It's a small bar next to the stage door of the Savoy theatre and hotel. In those days the basement of the bar was a live music venue, cramped, hot and very smoky but, fortunately for us, busy. At one of the gigs here I sensed for the first time that God might be challenging me about my ambitions. As I provided the backbeat, soaking up the atmosphere, watching people dance, others sitting at the bar knocking back the ale or enjoying a smoke, the Marshall stack screamed out the unmistakable tones of a Gibson SG guitar. But there was another voice cutting through the distortion, whispering, gently pointing a different path.

Was the God I dare to address as 'my Lord' really that important to me? Had my ambition to play drums become all-consuming to the point I had elevated it to a God-like position? Was this something I could let go of if I needed to? At the same time I started to look at people differently. I had always had a heart for the underdog, but I began to see beyond the drunk in the corner, the loudmouth with the girl on his arm, the bigot, the predator, the bully, the junkie, the freak and the geek. I began to see people as individuals whom God loved. I was no longer satisfied with being the short, sweaty guy at the back hiding behind his drums.

Several years later I stumbled across an album by a songwriter called Steve Camp that captured well the transition that had been taking place. Called *Justice*, the album had several tracks that challenged me immensely. One in particular, 'Don't tell them that Jesus loves them', laid down a challenge to put that love into practice and engage with people's pain and sorrow, far beyond lip-service. Gradually my faith in Christ became transformed from a noun into a verb. I realized that if I professed to be a follower of Jesus of Nazareth I had responsibilities not just to live responsibly but to make a deliberate move to the margins to make a connection with people who quite simply were never going to go anywhere near church.

This led to the inevitable. During our usual debrief after the Tuesday-night rehearsal, Mitch the guitarist and I sat at his parents' kitchen table talking long into the small hours. We'd often do this, discussing the music, the plans we had to make something of our musical dreams and the politics of keeping a band together. The band was going well, despite a few rifts that were beginning to occur; these were nothing to the tension I felt as I reordered my priorities. Band politics faded into the background as I laid my cards on the table and announced: 'You're probably not going to be able to get your head around this, but it's a bit of a God thing. I need to quit the band.'

It was nothing to do with the band I was being creative with, the style of music we were playing or the venues we performed in. There is nothing inherently evil about playing drums in a rock-and-roll band. To this day I love music; it continues to feed my soul and much of my life is filled with musicians and creative people. Not a day goes by when I don't allow myself to be carried by a song. You will not find a greater advocate for the voice of artistic expression, but for Sean Stillman at that moment in time it was about priorities deep within my soul, and an ambition needed to be sacrificed. There was to be another place where my identity would find security, a greater drive to motivate me and feed my soul.

4

The call

———◆———

This newfound hunger and desire to serve God, and be available to him, found some endorsement in those around me. Family and friends encouraged me to make enquiries with regard to training with a mission organization, or about more formal training for ministry. I opted to join a short-term mission team with British Youth for Christ, an organization that was close to my parents' hearts. Dad had been actively involved in YFC nationally and in Europe for many years. My middle name – Torrey – is in part a hat tip in the direction of Torrey Johnson, who co-founded YFC in the USA along with Billy Graham. The writer and preacher R. A. Torrey was another significant influence on my father.

Although only a short-term programme, this experience proved challenging for all the right reasons. I was still searching for confidence, and despite having a strong desire to serve God, much of my identity was still wrapped up in bikes and drums. But one summer's evening, as our mission team were hosting a gathering for young people in Coventry city centre, I was presented with an opportunity I never expected. A senior worker with YFC by the name of Roy Crowne took me to one side and said he wanted me to speak to the assembled crowd. Every part of my being was petrified at the thought of speaking in public anywhere, never mind to a crowd of people milling around who might or might not be interested.

I bit the bullet, and a few minutes later, in the grounds of Holy Trinity Church in Coventry, I told my story thus far. It wasn't one of those blood and guts conversion stories I had become familiar with growing up in church. My account was a long list of things I hadn't done – but it was an emerging tale of an ordinary life searching for identity, being changed by God's grace and mercy.

After I had done my piece and handed the microphone over to others much more confident, Roy and several others encouraged me over what I had said. They continued to encourage me to take opportunities and develop public speaking, but I was well out of my comfort zone. This was the boy who would hide behind people in class to avoid reading out loud. This was what my father was good at, not what I wanted to do. 'Are you sure God wouldn't rather I played drums instead?' was the response banging around my head.

I returned to Reading knowing things would be different, and committed myself to ongoing training with my home church, despite my lingering questions.

I had developed a taste for making a bit of a stand for my faith in Christ alongside my Christian biking mates. Together, as an assortment of misfits, we met for Bible study at the home of Ben and Jane Spiller, then we started to hang out at biker bars and began to organize our own events. The Spillers were pivotal in getting the original CMA Reading branch off the ground, the group that had embraced me and others so well. One of those early events was a Christmas charity ride, simply called a 'toy run'. You'll find toy runs – where bikers deliver gifts to children's projects and hospitals – happening all over the world.

There had been previous toy runs in Reading but the organizers of those had given up, so we decided to pick up the baton. We planned to do things in a similar format: arrange a meet point, ride together taking gifts to a suitable cause, then head somewhere afterwards for a social gathering at a bar or cafe. In addition we decided to create an opportunity to share something of our faith among our biker mates.

I had returned from the Coventry mission enthused, with a real fire in my belly to share the love of God with others. As I look back now I cringe, as my enthusiasm, although well meaning, was probably somewhat pushy and in some cases did more harm than good. I certainly regret that the last time I saw many old school friends was around this era and they must have thought I had gone mad. But however lacking in tact I was, my enthusiasm motivated me to bring a Christmas message to our biker mates who turned up to the toy run. This wouldn't come as a surprise, as we had advertised that there would be a talk as well as some hot soup at the end of the cold ride.

There's nothing worse than getting beaten around the head with a Bible when you least expect it. We should at least have the courtesy to warn people first! In a function room at the YMCA in Reading, a small and very cold band of bikers supped soup as I clambered onto the window sill to get everyone's attention. I thanked people for taking part and before awarding some prizes I gave a short summary of what it meant to us to be followers of Christ, encouraging those gathered there to consider the cause of Christ during that Christmas season. In the main it was well received – a bit of banter, which is great, and also some response. Some time later we discovered that that short message was to be the catalyst for change in one particular family. It was also the catalyst for me as a communicator and for our group of Jesus-following bikers to nail our colours to the mast.

Although that particular branch of the CMA disbanded after several of us moved to different locations, we have kept the toy run event going, organized by a group of friends together, supported by many more in the local community. Three decades on, this event can attract up to 2,000 participants each Christmas and benefits the children of Barnardo's projects and other welfare services throughout southern England. Bringing a short Christmas message of hope and faith in Christ remains a central and established part of the event and for some it's the only time they will hear or even listen to anything like it. It remains a wonderfully diverse close band of friends, some of strong faith, some of none, woven together in the service of others. Making a practical difference, meeting the needs of others, building wonderfully strong cohesive connections across the community and sharing our faith need not be complicated, and the Reading Toy Run is testimony to that.

These were important steps for us a group and me personally. Very early on I sensed that if God wanted to use me in this way, he was going to have to equip me. Nothing about my natural ability or academic training indicated that I should be able to stand up in front of a bunch of strangers and attempt to make a connection. But further opportunities came during the course of my year with my home church and among my mates on the bike scene. I began to lead youth meetings and preach in small local chapels, and received offers of ministry opportunities in a number of places, some of which seemed very appealing. Youth for Christ were putting a music and performing arts project together, which was tempting. They also had other opportunities in local centres and overseas in Singapore and New Zealand. But none of this resonated. I really felt I had to leave the musical aspirations behind me once and for all, and earnestly sought the desires that God had for me.

All this time my hunger for the Scriptures was very real. I had a deep commitment to regular devotional sessions of prayer and Bible study, entirely open to the possibility that through them God would challenge and lead me. Although people around me made very good suggestions on where the Lord might have me serve, I needed to know deep within my soul before I was going to commit myself to anything and with anyone. This knowing has proved essential in the long-term survival of not just my ministry but the very core of my faith. As the following years presented various challenges, my confidence in God's calling would hold me fast.

As a rough guide the thought process I went through and continue to follow is pretty straightforward and my prayers are often conversational.

OK, God, so you want me to give up playing the drums. Right, I understand the logic: it's you first, it's you I am trusting, it's you I want to serve, it's in you I have my identity, my worth and my value. But to be honest, I'm a bit thick and I want to know for sure whether giving up this ambition is the right thing. So on that basis, I'm going to keep this stuff to myself. I'm not going to talk about it with anyone, but I want you to confirm that what I'm sensing and hearing is you and not just a mad mix of emotions and skew-whiff dreams. So could you confirm this in ways and means and circumstances and through people who have no idea what we're talking about; direct me to Scriptures that will shed some light on the matter, again maybe through people who have no idea where my head is at, at the moment?

It may not be your standard liturgy for someone seeking discernment and spiritual direction, but it's honest, it's questioning and it's expectant.

If I have ever sensed the call of God, or the faintest whispers of his Spirit within my life, my default setting is to question it and to weigh it up. I began to keep a diary of the areas of my life I believed God was challenging me about and I started recording the Scriptures and comments that others brought into my life at the time independently. This desire to be sure stems from several influences.

I was brought up with a strong sense of a Jesus-oriented faith based on the Bible. My faith, or my brothers and sisters within the Church, should not make demands of me, or anyone, that are in conflict with what Jesus taught his friends. Therefore, I have a responsibility to know what Jesus taught and the responsibility to weigh up any hunches or advice from those around me in the light of his teaching. We may be surrounded by well-meaning people, all keen to give their opinions and advice, and we may have a strong emotional pull in one direction or another, but does it stack up with what Jesus taught?

Throughout this period of training and testing the waters with my home church, with Youth for Christ and with my mates in CMA, the sense of God's leading kept drawing me to the margins and particularly to those in the biking community. There were multiple mainstream church mission programmes and youth projects going on, but I was struggling to see the evidence that the Church was making tangible connections with marginalized and fringe groups. The more I delved into the Scriptures the more I discovered that the stories of Jesus were directed to the margins of his culture. He didn't hang out with popular people in popular places. The words were jumping out of the page at me. Jesus spent large parts of his time among misfits and lunatics, thieves and hookers, the sick and even the dead! In fact the only turn-or-burn sermons Jesus ever delivered were to the religious leaders of his day, whom he described as nothing short of a pretty-looking grave – looking great, but no life there whatsoever.

I eventually concluded that God was leading me towards those who were untouched by the usual expressions of church. It was my mates in the biking community and other fringe groups who needed to be the focus of my time and efforts. I continued to record these thoughts and prayers, keeping note of specific interactions with people or Scriptures that had any bearing on my thought process.

At the end of my time working at my home church, I agreed to attend an interview panel with YFC, as a candidate for their longer-term mission programmes. For one reason or another I couldn't make the date and it was rearranged on numerous occasions. By the time a suitable date was found, I had pretty much decided that this wasn't the route I was going to take, but I was still drawn to ride to London, where the interviews were taking place at Methodist Central Hall.

The meeting confirmed what I already thought. I needed to focus my energies elsewhere. I don't remember much else about the day, except the arrival of another interviewee who hadn't been able to make any of the previous dates either: a pretty girl from South Wales, dragging a suitcase behind her nearly as big as she was!

I returned to Reading and the drawing board, literally. I started back on short-term engineering drawing contract work, a few days a week, giving me enough to live on but also allowing me the time to explore options of developing mission opportunities within the biking community.

My time in CMA was proving beneficial both to me and to the club and I was appointed to a national leadership role. I put in more and more time on the road, taking other CMA members with me. We started to go to places we hadn't previously been to with a view to ministry, adding to the diary events hosted by back-patch clubs as well as the traditional enthusiast events and shows. If God was calling me to be some kind of expression of his hope and transformation among the biking community, then I needed to get in the mix, as inadequate as I felt, but I knew I couldn't do it alone. Early encounters in these formative years proved challenging and eye-opening – it was a steep learning curve – but gradually relationships were built amid a backdrop of bikes, bars, festival stages and the sometimes chaotic and unpredictable lifestyle that comes with the territory.

Eventually, having wrestled with God and still trying to understand where he wanted me to go and what he wanted me to do, I requested a meeting with the elders of my home church to present my story, my 'evidence' of a call to ministry. They very graciously gave me time to explain what was on my heart. I was finally prompted to make this request by a rather bizarre encounter. Although I was working on the drawing board a few days a week, I was finding I was getting more and more opportunities to speak at events, and increasing numbers of invitations from within the biker community to visit people in a variety of capacities including pastoral. All this was taking up a lot of time and I seriously began to think it was the moment to leave the security of the engineering work.

True to form, I laid everything out before God.

OK, Lord, this is the scenario. I'm happy with the fact that you are calling me to the margins. I can cope with that. I don't feel particularly gifted or equipped – in fact I feel pretty intimidated a lot of the time, but I'm prepared to accept that this is where you want me, and if you want me there, I figure you're going to be there also. But the reality is I can't do everything. I can't be on the drawing board, even if it is supporting me, so is this the time to pull the plug on this regular wage? I think it is, but I still continue to be a bit thick and I want to know for sure, so can you confirm this through ways and means and people that have no idea where my head is at?

A few days later I attended the regular Sunday gathering at my church. After the formal service concluded, a quiet, unassuming man handed me a slip of paper. Richard was one of the pianists in the church, a softly spoken guy and not someone I had down as one of those who appeared to have a hotline to God. He simply said, 'I was reading the Bible this morning and this passage came to my attention and I think I might need to suggest you take a look – sorry it's on this scrap of paper.'

I put the torn piece of notebook paper in my pocket and looked at it later at home. Richard had simply written in pencil, 'Sean – 2 Tim 4 v 5'. I opened up my Bible to the apostle Paul's second letter to the young man Timothy and much of the letter seemed so relevant to where I was at. None more so than the very verse Richard had written down. It reads: 'But you, keep your head in all situations, endure hardship, do the work of an evangelist, discharge all the duties of your ministry.' If there was going to be a verse in the Bible that said, 'Pull the plug on your secured income and get on with what I've told you to do', this was it. This wasn't the first time something like this had happened by any means, but these words, added together with everything else that was going on at this time, just seemed to confirm deep within my spirit what I needed to be doing with my life.

I sat down with the elders of the church and presented my story. I did so with confidence that I sensed the call of God and was prepared to carry the responsibility that came with it. I admitted having a lot of questions and certainly didn't feel overly adequate, but I was prepared to jump. This diverse group of leaders, some of whom had seen me grow up, were in agreement to endorse the call to mission that I believed God was leading me on. In due course they commissioned me, amid the congregation, in mission to the margins with a commitment to support me in prayer and some initial basic financial support. I continue to be thankful that they, and the church community, heard what I heard and supported me in it. Over time, especially on the days you feel wretched and want to give up and question whether you are just making it all up, you need these memories, these signposts along the way. As a young upstart, you need these collectives of godly wisdom to help guard, protect and support what you carry in your heart.

In my early years in ministry I had confidence in God's ability to lead and protect me, but I was dubious whether the Church, as a whole, was going to connect with the people I was hanging out with. My questions still burned about the relevance of the Church, of whichever flavour or denomination. The gulf between the Church and the fringes of our community appeared colossal. I was in danger of being in ministry but dropping out of institutional Church.

5

Blessed revolution

———◆◈◆———

By this time I was riding an old Yamaha XJ750, a four-cylinder shaft drive with a bullet-proof engine. I'd bought it with the compensation money from my accident a couple of years previously. Over the four years I had that bike, I rode over 100,000 relatively trouble-free miles. I covered every corner of the UK and most of Ireland on it, only dropping it once on a diesel spillage on the South Circular in London. As a single man with very few overheads, I was living off the smell of an oily rag and hardly ever at my parents' home. I was making connections all over the country at biking events and many of these gatherings started to feel like my parish.

Familiar faces in motorcycle clubs and traders at events would appear every few weeks in a different part of the country on the circuit of custom bike shows and meets. Gradually I was becoming accepted as an individual and as the CMA we began to break some new ground away from the traditional enthusiast rallies and more towards the fringe, lifestyle biking community. A four-page feature in a 1989 edition of the custom bike magazine *Back Street Heroes* was a significant milestone. In a piece simply titled 'The Son Set', the magazine's founder Steve Myatt quizzed me and two other CMA officers, Alan and Tony (who tragically died in a horrific accident two years later), about our faith and where we thought we might fit in the biking community.

The interview took place at the magazine's headquarters in Cheshire, affectionately referred to as The Towers. The three of us made the long ride there during a bitterly cold February, but it proved to be well worth while. Even now, all these years on, I don't think there's been a better feature in the UK bike press about Christian influence in the scene. Steve's sarcasm and wit were genuinely balanced by his curiosity, which reflected the attitude of many who were wondering who we were and what we were about. This experience enlightened me as to how influential effective use of the media can be, while also being acutely aware of the damage it can do. This was brought home to us when a national newspaper published an article on our group that included a description of how a couple of the guys had got beaten up. They used a very inappropriate headline which made things more complex in the aftermath of publication.

This was a significant period. We saw some fruit of our efforts within the scene, but there was also disappointment. Several guys and their families were profoundly influenced by our witness. Numerous people were coming to faith in Christ and these were exciting times of transformation. But this soon led to deep frustration; our mates from within the biking community were embracing our faith, but really couldn't put up with church. No matter how hard we tried to connect people with local contacts, it was like trying to communicate in a foreign language. The Church was speaking a different language from most of the people I knew and its symbols meant little to them. What was the point in bringing people to a point of faith if there was no chance of a communal expression of church that would make a tangible connection? When we were together on the road, it wasn't a problem. We spoke the same language and felt the same rain on our faces. When we dispersed to our own geographical areas, nobody in the church environment seemed to understand.

During this period, the late 1980s, I came across the work of an Australian biker and preacher, John Smith. He had founded a chapter of a club in Melbourne back in 1972 called God's Squad, off the back of an original group in Sydney a year or two before. John took the Melbourne end of the club and added a more radical edge to this on-the-road mission. He'd been a strait-laced Methodist but his faith underwent a radical rethink as the Jesus movement was taking off in the 1960s. He took a path from the Gospels that led him to the edges of society, out among the marginalized. At times the established Church gave him a wide berth as he began to challenge the comfortable and insular Christian experience that characterized that period. By the 1980s his reputation as a no-nonsense, passionate public communicator had reached beyond his native Australia and he was a regular speaker at the UK's long-running Christian music and arts festival, Greenbelt. I hunted down a copy of his book, *On the Side of the Angels*, which plotted his story. It wasn't difficult to find, as he seemed to be in the media a lot, including a television interview with the respected broadcaster David Frost, although it was a feature in *Bike* magazine that grabbed my attention first. Initially I was drawn to the fact that John Smith was into his bikes and into Jesus. What's more, Bono had endorsed the book and this was the time when U2's *Joshua Tree* album was hitting the headlines.

I got stuck into this book, and straight away it began to answer a lot of my questions about the Church and the way it connects with the wider community. He seemed to be addressing some of the questions I was asking. Any bike references soon faded into the background as I fed my soul on ideas I'd never really heard before, despite growing up within the Church. He enthused about mission that was deeper than people just making decisions to follow Christ. It wasn't about numbers and trophy-hunting and who had the best story. It should be about a radical call to follow this man Jesus of Nazareth. It was a call that challenged us to look at ourselves, our world and our mission differently. It dared to ask whether the prophetic voices were prepared to call the Church and governments to account. It was a call to embrace the arts.

All this was new to me. The arts were tolerated, though preferably avoided by and large, in my wider church experience and the only voices being peddled as prophetic seemed to want you to give them money or summon the spirit of a game-show host in putting on a performance. None of this 'speaking up for the rights of the poor and oppressed' had really featured for me. Caring for them, saving them from their plight, making sure they get to heaven before they die, yes; but John was daring to ask the question, 'Why have they no food and what are we going to do about it?' All of a sudden, my rock-solid black-and-white faith began to have shades of grey and even colour, not to mention a few holes. None more so than when I managed to get hold of a cassette tape of this Aussie speaking on the Beatitudes of Jesus.

Those eight beautiful phrases of Jesus that introduce the Sermon on the Mount in Matthew chapter 5 came as water in a dry land and fired in me a subsequent lifelong challenge to explore them, to bathe in them. I was amazed at how the journey from poverty of spirit to persecution opened up in a way I had never heard before. And if I was amazed at how it came alive as I listened, I was absolutely staggered that I had never heard it taught before.

Here I was, entering my early twenties, having grown up in church and found my own faith in Christ from a young age, listened to hundreds of sermons and sat through countless Bible study discussions and Sunday school classes, but I could not ever recall being taught on the Beatitudes. This was, after all, how Jesus introduced the path of discipleship to his band of brothers as they prepared to take to the road; these were the bare bones on which everything else would hang. Why had no one ever seen it as a priority in my whole church experience to teach me about them? Why had we trudged our way through the battles of the Old Testament and the finer points of Levitical law when there were these radical, subversive, seemingly impossible words of Jesus – words that did change the world, can change the world and should change the world if we take them seriously? I had heard a lot of talk about blessing from God and his kingdom, but not in the context that Jesus seemed to be speaking in these 'blessed' words. From that moment right up to now, not a day goes by when I don't consider the words of Jesus in the Beatitudes. Nearly 30 years on from listening to that cassette tape, I still read the Beatitudes with a fire in my belly, but now I do so with the additional experience of trying to work them out in a dirty, sometimes cruel world.

There are many who are far more qualified than me who can expound on the extent of their wisdom and insight. Indeed, enough to fill entire libraries. But allow me this enthusiastic indulgence to offer a mere taster to these words of Jesus of Nazareth in the hope that it encourages you to explore what lies in and beyond them, what lies within their mystery and subversiveness, and discover both the peace and the revolution that draws me closer still, yet catapults me to follow even when it seems folly.

Blessed are the poor in spirit, for theirs is the kingdom of heaven

The 'blessing' from God that Jesus spoke of was not about wealth, health or status, or anything temporal, unlike what many aspects of the Western Church would have us believe. In Matthew's Gospel (5.3–10) Jesus tells us exactly what it is to know the marks of his blessing in our lives and our communities. It's not about some inane plastic evangelical grin that hides a plethora of contradictions that we are afraid of letting out of the bag. It begins with poverty of spirit, permission to be ourselves with the assurance that Jesus is there alongside us – not standing at a distance pointing, condemning, judging, but sharing the very road we are travelling. 'Blessed are the poor in spirit' is how Jesus began his instruction to his friends, people who were living under the oppressive rule of the Roman Empire. You will know my embrace, my companionship and my love when you acknowledge who you are, with all your doubts, fears, broken bits, wobbly bits and screwed-up dirty bits. You will begin to know the very core of what it is to be loved by God, even when it appears that everything is against you, when you are at your most empty and most vulnerable, and not when you think you have nothing left to learn.

It won't be the medals on our chest but the scars on our soul that speak of poverty of spirit. Not only does the embrace of Christ become a gift, it becomes an understanding that the picture is far bigger than we could have imagined. The kingdom of heaven is granted as the rule of God within our soul, not some far-off land we hope to arrive at if we are good enough. If the journey begins with poverty of spirit there is room for all of us, except the proud, who see no need to empty their pockets of all that they cling to. It is an invitation to receive a gift, but it is a gift we have to reach out for, and this itself comes from a desire to make a change. We need to stand with open palms, not with our hands in our pockets or hidden behind our back, ready to receive an embrace that meets us where we are. To be open to receiving the gift of the kingdom of heaven is to be open to this righteous life, knowing how unrighteous we really are.

Blessed are those who mourn, for they will be comforted

Jesus encourages us to be mournful, which flies in the face of all those preachers and beige worship songs that tell us it's all about success and feeling good. Jesus actively wants us to embrace the blues. Living in the reality of the whole human experience means that we will know suffering. There has to be room for sorrow as we reflect on the carnage of our lives and the brokenness of the world we live in. If we are not traumatized by our collective inhumanity towards one another, which plays itself out on our news screens and in our neighbourhoods, we have to question what our faith consists of. Only when we know the trauma of loss and encounter an empathy that resonates deep within our soul can we know the deep comfort of God. The poor in spirit know how to sing the blues, because mourning is their response to what they see of the rebellion in their own heart and the pain they see around them in the lives of broken communities, in the greed of unjust governments and the horrors of human behaviour staring out in the hollow eyes of a stranger. If those who mourn will be blessed, it's with an embrace of grace and comfort and a conviction to keep going against all the odds, in the company of a Saviour known as a man of sorrows and acquainted with grief. Those in the trauma of mourning will not be left high and dry. We long for a better day to come – we hang on to the very hope of this – but with our fragile and sometimes exhausted faith we do well to fall into the arms of the love that will not let us go. Despite everything, we sing the blues and know that our cries are heard.

Blessed are the meek, for they will inherit the earth

Jesus continues his introduction to the journey by digging in the dirt rather than slinging mud around. He doesn't come out of the starting blocks with an obvious election-winning manifesto. He begins with poverty of spirit, encourages the blues and then advocates the concept of meekness. You are going to know I am with you, right there alongside you, when you embrace all the earthiness of life. Meek, humble people know that life stinks. They are not afraid to get their hands dirty and make themselves at home amid the chaos and disorder flung up from the spinning wheels of life struggling for traction. As Jesus bathed his disciples' feet he intimately and affectionately celebrated their very existence. He literally got down in the dirt, writing at the feet of a woman caught in adultery and also those of the religious leaders who were about to execute her. He carried a gift within his heart that money couldn't buy. Meekness is too often seen as weakness; I have never heard, at any funeral I have been present at, a tribute that celebrated meekness: 'and the best thing about our departed brother was that he was a meek person'. It is not a virtue real men want to be labelled with, or an attribute of people who want to get ahead and make something of their lives.

Meekness, however, is a strength that's worth aspiring to. I can think of few other attributes that I would need or want more. Far from being weak, shallow, a pastel shade in the distance, meekness challenges power in strength like the silence of a sunset; it's humility turned up to maximum yet doesn't raise its voice or make a fuss. It's vanity's worst nightmare; it's faith as a verb in the grimmest of environments that isn't looking for applause. Meek people carry a wealth within their soul that radiates the spirit of Jesus. They fear nothing and no one. They lead by example and stand before pharaohs, Goliaths, warmongers, politicians, bullies and betrayers to demonstrate, with dirty hands, how life can be radically different. Meekness has an uncanny way of disarming the most intimidating of aggressors and the meek have the knack of being blessed with a wealth in their soul that quite simply cannot be bought.

Blessed are those who hunger and thirst for righteousness, for they will be filled

The accumulation of possessions, wealth, knowledge, experiences and status is a curse of our culture. We gorge ourselves on all these things that leave us wanting more. Next on Jesus' manifesto comes a statement at the very core of what drives us. It begs of us an answer to the question: what is it that feeds my very soul? Where do I get my fill? What do we hunger and thirst for? What can't we live without for our very survival? Jesus spoke to his followers in the dry heat of a parched land. They knew what it was like to be thirsty, what difference a few drops of water make in a dry mouth on a scorching day. To know the contentment of the soul, the quenching of our questions of what life is really all about – this blessing comes when we pursue righteousness and justice.

It comes when we don't see ourselves more highly than we ought, and we advocate the rights of the poor and oppressed.

It calls us to serve and speak out and acknowledges that the world does not revolve around us. We are called to make a difference and are granted contentment, knowing that we have sought to do the will of the Lord. This blessing challenges our ambitions and questions our motivations. It becomes a matter of discovering what the Lordship of Christ means to us in the routine of everyday life. It keeps our ego in check and prevents us from ascending a pedestal either of our own making or one that others may wish to build for us. For those who hunger and thirst after righteousness, the adulation of the crowd is an empty cup, for there is a silent contentment in the certainty that God sees all things and knows the hearts of all people.

The way of Christ gives us nothing to brag about, but it nourishes the deepest part of who we are in Christ and sustains us on our journey, whatever we encounter. Later in the Sermon on the Mount, Jesus says that we should make the pursuit of his kingdom and righteousness our first desire, and in consequence his obedient followers will know what it is to live life without want (Matthew 6.25–34).

Blessed are the merciful, for they will be shown mercy

The mercy of God, and that shown by those we share our life with, is a gift to be treasured. In the absence of mercy, life would soon descend into chaos. The introduction of mercy into a situation trumpets that grace has entered the building and sends the strongest possible signal that life can be radically different. It is possible for transformation to happen if we ourselves are prepared to take the risk of daring to show mercy. Blessed is the person who shows mercy. Blessed is the person who dares to go down the road of demonstrating that there is another way. Where we make room for love, for forgiveness, for grace, for standing alongside and in solidarity with the 'accused, misused, strung out ones and worse' that Bob Dylan wrote of in 'Chimes of Freedom', we present the possibility of change, the possibility of transformation – of a person, a community, a nation or an entire culture. After all, what right do we have to stand before God and expect mercy when we have not been prepared to wrestle with showing this same gift to others?

Blessed are the pure in heart, for they will see God

'OK,' says Jesus to his travelling companions, 'you want to see God? I'll tell you how you'll get a glimpse. He'll start coming into focus when you take seriously sorting the inside stuff – you know, what we've just been talking about: poverty of spirit, embracing the blues, meekness, feeding your soul on what does you and others justice, wrestling with mercy. Begin to get a handle on this and you'll start to see God all around you.'

The trouble we have when we hear references to the heart, such as in this beatitude, is that we automatically think of the emotional aspect wrapped up in heart imagery and references. When Jesus spoke these words, 'heart' was not used to describe the source of emotional whims. The emotional centre was in the guts, from which we derive the expression 'gut feeling'. The heart meant what we now generally refer to as the head. In this context, the heart is really mission control. It's where decisions of what's right and what's wrong are made – based not on how they make you feel, but on what you know to be true. It's where rational, well-thought-out choices are decided on, the fertile soil where our virtues, our codes, our ethics grow and mature. The heart is where we make calculated decisions of judgement, and where we allow the light from the windows of the soul to illuminate the world around us. But that seeing is continually thwarted by the obstacles we place in the way, those planks of self-righteous superiority that we convince ourselves give us some God-given right to pass judgement on the specks of sawdust in another's eye.

It's only when we truly begin to embrace sorting what's inside us that God comes into sharper focus, as we remove the planks that obscure our vision. Purity of heart is the beautiful gift of how God the Father sees us in the light of his Son's sacrifice – stain-free, a soul washed in the most miraculous of detergents. It's the outworking of our faith by living with gratitude in the light of this, which enables us to see where God's Spirit is abiding and at work in the most unlikely of places. Eugene Peterson translates this verse brilliantly in *The Message*: 'You're blessed when you get your inside world – your mind and heart – put right. Then you can see God in the outside world' (Matthew 5.8).

Blessed are the peacemakers, for they will be called children of God

Just when the disciples thought it couldn't get any more bizarre, Jesus has the audacity to suggest that they should be advocates of peace. Here they were, a bunch of sometimes argumentative misfits, which included at least one extremist, Simon the Zealot. He wanted to overthrow the occupying Romans, possibly by force. He sat alongside Matthew the tax-collector, who had earned a dodgy living prior to this road trip, in cahoots with the aforementioned Romans. I am sure there were many animated discussions within Jesus' small band of followers as they wrestled with their extremely varied social and political opinions. Regardless of what is happening on the world stage, keeping peace within the community remains a challenge.

When the Christian faith has been a cosy bedfellow to so much division, conflict and war throughout history, it's with a deep sense of heartache that I read these words of Jesus. How can they possibly be interpreted any other way than being about peace? A tangible, identifiable mark of claiming to be a follower of Jesus Christ of Nazareth, the Prince of Peace, is that of being a peacemaker. Being a disciple of Jesus meant being prepared to walk into the middle ground and bring reconciliation. A peacemaker is required to put preconceived ideas, hasty judgements, rumours, dubious intelligence operations and previous history to one side and say, 'Let's talk'. There may be differences, and perhaps the stench of conflict on the horizon, but I'll put my own life on the line and walk out into the middle ground and try for reconciliation. Down through history, many Christians have been prepared to stand in the gap and work for peace and reconciliation at great personal cost. Some Christian denominations particularly stand out as championing the cause for peace, such as the Quakers and the Mennonite tradition.

But there is the harsh reality that being a peacemaker is not an attribute that many associate with the Church. Maybe we need to seriously reflect and act upon the previous six beatitudes. Is it the absence of these qualities that makes us so hopelessly inept at being agents for peace? If life continues to be based around me, myself and I, then I'll always have something to defend. But if what I do have of any material wealth I hold lightly, if the treasures that mean the world to me are written within the scars of my soul, then what have I got to fight for and defend? Those who stand out as belonging to God carry within their hearts a desire for peace and reconciliation, which spurs them to make a stand, going against the tide of popular opinion, challenging them to cross borders, to earn the right to speak and make their voices count. The loudest voice from within the Church should not be one of chaos, conflict and confusion, but of reason, reconciliation and peace.

Whether it be on the world stage or in the dysfunctional family home, the mark of being an agent for peace is one that Jesus called blessed. As Jesus' battered body hung, and he relinquished his spirit, it's no wonder that one observer commented, 'Surely this was the Son of God.' The ultimate act of reconciliation, of border crossing, of bridging the greatest divide and of making the option of peace with God accessible and freely available, was made possible not by peace through superior firepower, but a life laid down amid humiliation, degradation, accusation and isolation.

Blessed are those who are persecuted because of righteousness, for theirs is the kingdom of heaven

It's no wonder that before he gets to the end of his pre-road-trip pep talk, Jesus speaks of persecution. A more subversive, counter-cultural, topsy-turvy manifesto for revolution you will not find anywhere. The peace that Jesus brought had a price, and any peace that his followers may choose to make a stand for may also carry a price. To finish his introductory mandate to his travelling companions by exhorting the virtues of persecution must have seemed odd. I don't know how long he spent explaining it all. He must have needed to repeat it, over and over. It's taken me a lifetime of grappling with it and I am still being challenged by these same words.

'Blessed are those who are persecuted because of righteousness, for theirs is the kingdom of heaven.' The part of that statement that has come to resonate most with me is the 'because of righteousness' phrase. Jesus isn't talking about persecution resulting from hypocrisy, double standards, greed or disrespectful attitudes. Being held to account for ramming the Bible down someone's throat or for being an obnoxious loudmouth is not persecution. There's a big difference between taking a beating for being insensitive, selfish and greedy, and taking a beating 'because of righteousness'. There's an air of inevitability about what Jesus brings to his friends in conclusion. If they take these words of his seriously, and desire to put them into practice, it will cause a stir. It will do more than ruffle a few feathers, because these words fly in the face of so much of what our world has become comfortable with. Where there are the people of Christ there should be a counter-cultural challenge to greed, selfishness and hatred. The powerful should be nervous of the church community; and the church community should not live in fear of holding powers to account with integrity, boldness, love and a righteous spine that will not buckle. Persecution will follow where there is a righteous stand, threatening the appetites of the powerful. But where there is persecution there is Christ also, and the knowledge that he is alongside and within those who walk that painful and humiliating road to freedom.

The Beatitudes that John Smith had switched me on to were a revelation and a revolution in my soul. That old cassette tape ignited a fire that still burns; to say that these words of Jesus have transformed my faith in Christ is an understatement. It was like a whole new section of the map had been discovered that put everything else into perspective – the part of the map that indicated true north and pointed to a place of completeness. Whatever the world may throw at us, there's a fixed point in the chaos.

The word 'blessed' remains a challenge to translate into English from the Greek. Some translate it simply as 'happy', but it has to be more than that. R. T. France, theologian and expert in Matthew's Gospel, has offered helpful insight as I have continued to explore the depths of the Beatitudes. He draws attention to the Welsh language translation of the word 'blessed', which is *gwyn eu byd*. It means 'white is their world', and for me that evokes a sense of 'all is well with my soul'. It adds an additional depth as I try to understand the richness of what it is to be blessed by God.

John Smith's exploration of the Beatitudes changed me. It was no longer about me and any talent, gift or ability that I might or might not bring. It was no longer about whether an experience of church was good or bad, or about a search for an emotional high or putting on a good performance to keep up appearances. It was about starting at the beginning, with poverty of spirit – a declaration of my weaknesses, failures, insecurities and quirks, but with a deeper understanding that God knew all this and he liked me anyway. It was continuing with a journey exploring what it means to be fully human in the light of the bigger picture the Gospel writers refer to as the kingdom of heaven.

Many years later, I had the opportunity to commission seven artists to produce their own interpretations of the eight

Beatitudes. The stunning collection of paintings, sculpture, poetry and print that resulted stand testimony to the timeless challenge of these words of Jesus of Nazareth that have an ability to cross cultural borders and continue to issue a subversive cry for life to be lived, differently.

I conclude this chapter with the one piece of artwork from that collection I can share with you in the pages of a book. I wish I could share them all, but it is an honour to set down here Stewart Henderson's beautiful poem on Jesus' words about meekness.[1]

Meek abundance

How precise the fermentation,
and delicate the savour
of meekness;

elixir
of distilled strength
and transparency;

this slight fortune
causes the bitter empires
of passing Herods
to rage and slay,
as the meek,
like lions disguised as butterflies,
choose not to render, in return;

for, to be meek
is not to excel at appeasement
or to dissolve
into muted compliance,

meekness, like justice,
abides,
brooding with charity

Blessed revolution

counting the certain steps
of the approaching Pure day

beware the meek,
they have supped
the crystal chalice

and even when they are disappeared
and thought extinct,
they return complete
with perpetual joy,
their speech succinct

6

My confession

I was sitting in the front seat of a van next to a 19-year-old occasional prostitute. It was dark, the rain was torrential, deafening on the van roof, and the wipers flapped from side to side punctuating our conversation.

Lizzy had followed her mother in replicating a life clinging to multiple addictions and dysfunctional temporary relationships. She thought she might be pregnant again and asked me if I had any children. 'Sure, I have four kids, and one wife,' I answered. 'Yeah, but they're not all with the same missus, are they?' Lizzy retorted. I will never forget the look of utter disbelief on her face as I confirmed that all four of my children were indeed with my one wife. Her mouth just hung open, revealing a few tooth stumps rotting from the effects of her drug abuse. For once, the usually mouthy Lizzy was lost for words.

The passenger door opened and Scott, her on-off boyfriend, climbed up into the remaining passenger seat, having put his bag in the back of the van. ''Ere, Scott, Sean's got four kids all with the same missus!' 'Bloody hell, that's different,' said Scott, as he wiped the rain off his face. 'Did you break her in then, or did she break you in?' Lizzy quizzed further with a genuine fascination and a matter-of-factness that only a sex therapist or a prostitute would have. 'We were each other's first, and only,' I replied with a little more tact. 'It's only ever been the two of us.'

For Lizzy, this was a completely alien concept, belonging to a different world from the one she had been part of for as long as she could remember. For a puzzling moment, she tried to imagine what it would be like, but she just couldn't. Sex was frequently little more than currency, first to fuel her mother's addiction and then to pay for her own. Bruises, abuse, rape, pregnancy and prison had become the unwanted interest on a debt she couldn't pay, and the closest experience she had of intimacy these days was sharing a needle, a spoon and can of Special Brew with Scott. I dropped them off at their squat. Scott climbed through the upstairs window and came down to open the front door for Lizzy, then they disappeared inside to get shelter for the night.

When the apostle Paul wrote his beautiful manifesto on love to the emerging church community in Corinth, he did so because love was an alien concept there too. In Roman-influenced Greek Corinth, love certainly wasn't patient, kind or thinking of the best for others; it wasn't affirming and it certainly wasn't beautiful. It was selfish and took what it could get. Roman men were expected to be as dominant in their sexual activity as they were while on duty as soldiers. Whether it was sex with women or men or the systematic rape of child slaves, theirs was a code that thrived on power and coercion, was steeped in inequality and in which promiscuity was applauded. It was into this context that the apostle wrote:

> Love is patient, love is kind. It does not envy, it does not boast, it is not proud. It is not rude, it is not self-seeking, it is not easily angered, it keeps no record of wrongs. Love does not delight in evil but rejoices with the truth. It always protects, always trusts, always hopes, always perseveres. Love never fails.
> (1 Corinthians 13.4–8)

I would dare to add, 'Love doesn't ask: what will I get out of this?'

This mandate for a new way of loving flew in the face of everything Roman power stood for, and expressed a very different code from that instilled in this and other cities by the ancient Greeks. It wasn't popular then, and would have contributed to fears that the Christian community could destabilize Rome. In its fullest flowering, it isn't popular now. Paul's words have become an acceptable and welcome reading at weddings today, even of those who do not profess faith, and are held up as ideals. But it requires serious commitment to apply them with the radical intent Paul had in mind.

Far from being prudish, offering an outdated killjoy ethic or a tick-box list of restrictive rules, the words offer a radical alternative, a new way of loving, a new way of flourishing within a framework of mutual respect and covenant commitment rather than one based on dominance and fear. This was a rebellious, counter-cultural path that threatened those lording power over vulnerable people. For the abused and discarded, Paul's vision offered liberation.

The virtue of chastity and the exercise of self-control over carnal desires remains as alien a concept now as it was when Paul advised the Corinthian church. It seems an unnatural way to behave in response to the most natural of urges known to humanity. Why deny yourself? Is the fear of God's wrath that strong? In my case, growing up within a strongly religious environment had the potential to foster multiple qualifications in guilt, and generous portions of shame if any secrets got out. The tension of having to behave how others expected me to was gradually replaced by a deliberate choice to live differently, not reluctantly, and came with a liberating confidence that my identity did not rest on any kind of sex-cess or failure.

My decision to stay chaste until marriage wasn't a result of there being no opportunity; rather it was a genuine response to a deeply held desire to do the right thing, to live righteously. Two of the visible fruits of that are love and self-control. The desire to live in a certain way that was honourable before God became a stronger pull than any notion of living with compromise. But eventually, the sometimes lonely wait came to an end. The girl with the suitcase I'd seen at the interview at Westminster Central Hall a few years previously had kept reappearing in my life with increasing frequency and mutual fascination.

When I first briefly met Jayne at the interview, I was intently focused on setting my sails vocationally for the years ahead. The search for any temporal relationships or a life partner were simply not on my radar. I didn't allow myself the freedom to be sidetracked, nor did I want to risk the emotional fallout of a failed relationship. How blinkered I was!

Our paths crossed on several occasions, and then Jayne's brother Chris came to work at my home church in Reading for a year as part of a youth team placement. As siblings, Jayne and Chris clearly thought the world of each other, and their mutual appreciation was very special to see. Over time I got to know them both independently. Jayne, though the younger of the two, had been the first to work in Christian youth ministry and easily took to interacting with young people. She was a sensitive communicator, and young teens were obviously comfortable in her company. She was non-threatening, and fun to be with.

Like me, Jayne had been a shy child with a painful experience of school, but she had latterly found her voice and expression in many aspects of performing arts. A lifetime on, she is never more fully alive than when she is performing, whether it be Shakespeare on the stage or hitting harmonies perfectly in the music studio on a vocal track. On stage she holds nothing back, and her off-stage shyness is replaced with fearless confidence. When we first met, Jayne was particularly passionate about and gifted in the art of classical mime. She had the confidence to do not only stage work but also street theatre, captivating a crowd with myriad expressions and movements silently telling a story. At one point there was even an invitation open for her to further this particular discipline in Canada.

When we first met I wasn't looking for love; in fact if anything I was looking to avoid it. But there was something about this warm, engaging girl from South Wales with the cute accent and a black leather jacket! Her post-punk mischievous nature and the sparkle in her eyes hinted at a sassy young woman cutting her own groove, and so it was, in a little black and white spotty dress, that she danced into my world.

In the heat of summer, it is easy not to appreciate the warmth of the sun when there's work to be done. We block it out with hats and sunglasses and gravitate to the shade when it gets too distracting. Hiding from any rays of love's potential, I had kept myself well and truly in the shade at the time of that interview. But now, because I had much more confidence and assurance, Jayne had my full attention. I could not ignore the magnetism of our attraction.

The beauty I had been hiding myself from was now as inviting as the setting sun over still waters. It was throwing a blanket of kaleidoscope hues across the sky while the sun silently slipped from the heavens and kissed the sea. For fleeting moments the horizon disappeared as the sky and sea became one magical canvas, and its caress gathered me in.

No sooner had the sunset promise embraced us in its warmth, the storm clouds gathered. Our engagement was imminent, but ambushed by tragedy. Just days after I proposed to Jayne, her brother Chris died in a horrific car accident. Nothing prepares a family for this kind of pain and nothing anyone can say or do can ease it, change it or remove it.

It was therefore against a backdrop of heartache and grief that Jayne and I were married on a crisp winter's day in her beloved home city of Swansea. We had waited for each other, with each other, and been faithful to our shared belief in the sacredness of marriage. We had sought to honour God in singleness, and now we sought to honour God in our marriage with promises and declarations of love, faithfulness, honour, care and cherishing. We made those promises like every other couple, thinking that we knew everything there is to know. We stood there with our suitcases of hopes, dreams, heartaches, fears and a desire to serve our God together. Like in any marriage, the discovery of the contents of our emotional, spiritual and psychological baggage would bring all the highs and lows of human experience.

Writing over a quarter of a century later, I have a confession to make as I open one of my own suitcases. I don't believe I have kept the vows I made to my bride as well as I ought to have done. Many an autobiography has sold on the prominent storylines of a cheating partner, lies and infidelity, but it's not the vow of faithfulness I need to be reminded of. It is the vow of cherishing.

That promise – to make your partner feel special and doted on with affection – is a promise I have frequently failed to keep. It's not intentional. I adore my wife; I am just not very good at demonstrating it. This is nothing new – it's like an illiteracy of intimacy, a language I needed to learn to develop. But I've been a tough nut to crack. My inner self is fraught with insecurities and fears of failure. It represses emotion and develops calluses where there should be tenderness. There is often silence when there should be words, and indeed words where there should be silence, and distance where there should be touch. There are missed opportunities where there should be attention. I have frequently cursed the weight and awkwardness of this suitcase.

When I think of Lizzy and our conversation in the van, I am reminded of U2's track 'Every Breaking Wave'. It speaks of the shipwrecked souls of this world that become accustomed to a bankruptcy of intimacy. But it's not just the Lizzys of this world, the obvious shipwrecked souls, who are bereft of the ability to receive affection and affirmation and also unable to express how they truly feel towards someone.

My upbringing gave me a language for what is right and wrong, a spine and a steel to not give up, a desire to live simply and to be faithful in all things. But it is Jayne who has taught me about tenderness, empathy, intimacy, sensitivity, about what it is to develop, not repress emotional language and expression. It is my wife and the home we have created with our four unique, zany, creative, loving children that have taught me most about what it is to be fully human.

Without this galaxy of illumination, and if I had been left to my own callused dysfunction instead, I don't know what kind of husband, father, friend and pastor I would have been. I am still learning to cherish. Every day I am still thankful to watch the sun slip from the sky, kiss the sea and feel the warmth of its embrace.

7

Colours

———•─•———

Tracking down John Smith himself proved to be far more difficult than getting hold of the Aussie's books. By 1989, after my second reading of *On the Side of the Angels*, I had started to make some enquiries to meet with John. I was intrigued by his Melbourne-based motorcycle club, God's Squad, and I had a gut feeling that I would be bringing this club to the UK, rather than create something new.

They seemed to have an established, respected and accepted ministry among the motorcycle clubs in Australia and this was a subculture that I was genuinely feeling drawn to minister among. I was very committed to my role within the Christian Motorcyclists Association, but I had this nagging doubt, despite CMA's valuable ministry among the broader motorcycle enthusiast scene, that it was not going to be the vehicle to engage meaningfully with the colours-wearing motorcycle clubs. ('Colours' are a motorcycle club member's back patch. They are earned over an extended period of time, not bought or given away cheaply. They are a tribal identity and symbolic of ultimate commitment to their particular club. Many bikers wear insignias of all kinds, but not many wear 'colours'. Those who do are part of a subculture that speaks of brotherhood, honour and courage.) I became convinced that an extremely dedicated Christian club, passionate about building meaningful relationships, was needed in that specific community. I made enquiries among friends in some of these clubs where I had already formed relationships, and began introducing the idea of starting God's Squad in the UK.

While what you ride isn't the be-all and end-all, it does help if you have a bike that's relevant to the subculture. In this case it's predominantly about Harley Davidsons, preferably modified, customized ones, not something straight out of the factory. Here began a journey that has seen me travel many miles on Harleys. I began as I meant to go on, aiming to prove that you don't need to spend a fortune to ride this most famous of motorcycle marques. I built my first Harley from odd bits I had accumulated. A 1980 Ironhead Sportster engine, bought with my last gig as a drummer, fitted into a rigid 1962 frame. A single seat, minimal electrics, straight through drag pipes and flat black finish kept everything simple as well as cost-effective.

There are many useful aspects to building a project bike. You learn a lot by getting on with the job in the workshop, especially if like me you are a bit cack-handed with spanners. With some good, patient mates lending their oversight it is not only a great way to learn but a great environment to get to know each other. Making brackets from scraps of metal off-cuts, sourcing parts from breakers' yards – and, of course, you have a reason to hang out in the local independent Harley store. In one shop I struck up a conversation with a member of staff who happened to belong to the local club. I bounced the idea around of starting a Christian back-patch club. His response was courteous but frank: 'We don't care what you do. As far as we're concerned you are persona non grata – we don't take you seriously. We don't care what you do.' It gave me a lot to think about. The door wasn't closed, but it wasn't what you'd call a resounding endorsement! It did demonstrate, however, that I and whoever was going to take the step with me had a lot to learn and do, if we were to have any impact.

Eventually I got an opportunity to meet up with John Smith. He had been coming over to Greenbelt festival for a few years, and to other festivals in Holland. He was a sought-after speaker and fortunately by this time had acquired the services of a manager. Steve Drury did a brilliant job. He ensured that John was organized, looked after and making the most of every opportunity. He was the one who arranged for John to be interviewed by David Frost on the UK *Sunday Breakfast Show* as well as many other media and radio slots off the back of his books and speaking. But, of course, having a good manager can make it difficult for others to get near. I was fortunate as John was booked to speak at a church in Reading. A local friend, Heather Curnow, was organizing the event and she had worked in Steve Drury's office in Sydney for a while. That was enough to create the opportunity to meet.

Over the next few years John and I kept in touch. We met on numerous occasions, sometimes in transit in airport lounges, sometimes at festivals. Then in 1991 I got the opportunity to go on a ten-day UK tour with John, Cardiff-based song-writer Martyn Joseph and Lowell Sheppard, then the National Director of Youth for Christ, who were organizing the tour. I took a couple of friends along with me and we shifted gear, helped out in whatever way we could and provided a radical Harley chop for the stage set. The 'Where the Rubber Hits the Road' tour in the spring of 1991 was pivotal for me. Hearing the stories of Jesus on the road blown wide open by Smithy each night in a different town and seeing his sincere and street-level approach to talking with people after the meetings was something different. He wasn't the big-shot preacher keeping an audience at a distance; his style was a much more vulnerable way of communicating. He was giving something of himself, baring his soul in stories with a sharpness and depth of intellect that was refreshing. The Jesus of the Gospels was becoming more alive and more radical in my understanding. The beginnings of God's Squad into Europe, therefore, emerged partly from a genuine sense of calling to bring it into being as a mission among motorcycle clubs, and partly from my own deepening relationship with the message of Jesus in the Gospels.

By the summer of 1992 it had become clear that I needed to move on from CMA. Jayne and I had married and were living in Reading; we were also wanting to set in motion some concrete plans. In August that year John Smith was back in the UK for Greenbelt. Jayne and I travelled to the Greenbelt headquarters in London to pick up John and his wife Glena. We returned to our tiny attic flat for a meal, then went on to Ben and Jane Spiller's place for what can best be described as a Bible study and chat. I had invited about 40 people who might, in any way, be interested in God's Squad or what John had to say. Folks rode from all over the country to be there. We squeezed into their lounge, overflowing out into the garden, and listened intently to Smithy, firing questions and talking late into the night.

Although God's Squad did not officially start until a couple of years later, in my mind these were the first shoots. The Spillers' lounge, where for several years we had prayed and studied the Bible as a local CMA branch, was where I knew for sure that we going on an adventure together – me, Smith and anyone else we could find. John saw it the same way and was keen to make mention of this gathering in his interview with *The Times* that covered his UK visit that summer.

Gradually a group of us started to take to the road with a view to forming the first God's Squad chapter outside of Australia. Unbeknown to me at the time, God's Squad, despite being a well-established club in Melbourne, had gone through a crisis a few years before, at the time of my first contact with John. It had in fact reduced to just a handful of members and there was a lot of heartache and soul-searching. At exactly the same time as this fresh-faced young Englishman was being challenged, similar challenges were being encountered on the other side of the world. A group in Tasmania had become a chartered chapter of God's Squad as a result of initial contact with John's on-the-road missions and his radical call to follow Jesus seriously. Similar momentum was gathering in Sydney,

Brisbane and in Wellington, New Zealand. There was a renewed enthusiasm and vision in Melbourne, but would it extend all the way to Europe?

Starting a new chapter of a club in a new area is always a challenge. It can be a political minefield as well as a logistical challenge in the same country, never mind another continent. During a subsequent meeting with John, this time at Heathrow airport while he was in transit between Holland and home, he recorded an interview with me to take back to the club in Melbourne. I quizzed him about many areas of club life, including the tensions that can arise from purposefully living with Christian integrity amid a subculture that often holds very different values.

Over the next two years I continued to build on the relationship with John and God's Squad. Jayne and I spent some time in Australia, partly to find out more about God's Squad, partly to look at the numerous associated ministries that had developed out of and alongside the club. Seminars had been conducted in over 3,000 schools in Australia over a 20-year period, and there was a developing work with young offenders and a street-level community church full of marginalized misfits, affectionately known by some as a church for the medicated, St Martin's in Collingwood, Melbourne.

Jayne's creativity was already broadening my appreciation for the arts and John significantly contributed to my interest in the role of artist in a community. I had grown up in a church environment of bland bare walls where the arts were held at a distance, unless an image was legitimized by having a Bible verse tacked on.

John described the arts as the nerve ends of a culture. There were questions to be asked of society, souls searching to make sense of chaos, protests needing to rise up and voices needing to be heard. We needed to listen to the sometimes chaotic voice and troubled life of the artist if we wanted to make serious connections with the culture we were living in. Smithy not only opened up the Gospels and the arts, he opened our eyes and ears to see where God was already at work long before we turned up. There was much to see and experience. But on our arrival in Australia, it all nearly fell at the first hurdle.

Our first port of call wasn't Melbourne. We were to join a team for a week in another city, and while it was great listening to John speak we didn't feel welcomed by everyone on the team. To this day I couldn't tell you whether it was intentional, but it was an awkward and uncomfortable situation. There were some personal upsets that caused us to question whether our long trip down south was going to be worth it. We hadn't really had any contact with God's Squad yet, but that was coming. It was Jayne's birthday the day we flew into Melbourne, and we decided that if Melbourne turned out to be a similarly negative experience, then we would be heading home in 24 hours.

Fortunately, it was a different story. The now resurgent and enthusiastic Melbourne chapter made us very welcome and we completed our trip encouraged to pursue bringing God's Squad to the UK. We were also open to the other aspects of ministry we had witnessed. Returning home – we had recently moved to the East Midlands – Jayne continued her schools and youth work, particularly using her creativity in classical mime and acting. She also trained for her teaching certificate in speech and drama. I took to the road when I could while over time forming a group that would be the beginnings of God's Squad in the UK.

Alongside this, in between leaving CMA and beginning God's Squad, I had started something called Bibles for Bikers. It was a simple idea. I booked advertising space in lifestyle motorcycle magazines like *Back Street Heroes*, offering a Bible and a user's guide, posted free of charge. As a result of the relationship I had built up with *BSH* over the years at shows and events, they initially dropped their own house adverts for a few months and gave me free advertising space to see if the idea had any mileage. My mate Spike came to the fore and between us we created a series of adverts that went along the lines:

> Bibles for Bikers – It's No Joke! Read the world's most read book, free. Drop us a line and we'll send you a free copy of the world's most read book in a modern translation and a user's guide. We promise we won't post you any other junk and no plonkers in suits will knock on your door.

From the outset, we were receiving about 30 requests per issue, with about one in ten choosing to continue contact via a correspondence course. Bibles for Bikers ran for several years, distributing several thousand Bibles; we only discontinued it because of rising advertising costs and falling magazine sales. My old mates in CMA, however, picked up the baton and developed it on a different angle and in partnership with the Bible Society, producing the *Biker's Bible, Manual for Life*. Every now and then I still receive a letter or email from someone who received one of the original Bibles we sent out in the 1990s.

Bibles for Bikers respondents remained anonymous unless further contact was requested. Developing God's Squad, however, was definitely face to face. I had been attending motorcycle shows and events for years but now the dynamic was about to change. In wanting to establish God's Squad in the UK, we were riding into new territory, literally. At that time in the UK there were no other Christian motorcycle clubs wearing colours. Putting colours up is fraught with complex political issues. If you want to maintain and develop relationships with as many clubs as possible, which we did, then being open, honest and upfront had to be the norm. There was no room for hidden agendas, ego trips or freeloaders.

If we were to hit the road as a club, I needed to know who wanted to be involved and that we were certain of our motives and sure that we were called by God. By now I had experienced all the aspects of the bike scene I love and also seen some of its ugly aspects. There's a camaraderie within the bike scene that doesn't exist in many other places in Western culture. It's much more than being part of a golf club or a social group. It has a fiercely tribal mentality and attracts a huge diversity of personalities. Many of the clubs are structured within tight boundaries and discipline codes, which means that they can offer space and opportunities for some men who wouldn't fit anywhere else. (And it was always men: clubs are very male-dominated.)

Over the years I've met a number of semi-psychotic men with a multitude of complex issues who have only managed to stay alive and remain functional because of the disciplined structure of the club they are in. They know that if they screw up, they're out of the club and that doesn't bear thinking about; for some it's all they've got. Others have been given the opportunity of developing significant leadership skills and have proved themselves to be exceptionally gifted and charismatic in these roles.

As with any close-knit and tightly disciplined group there is opportunity for abuse, and for manipulative dictatorial egos to exert unhealthy and destructive influence on what initially might be a cohesive unit. Keeping the rules and playing your part are vital for the tribe to function. It shouldn't be surprising, then, that motorcycle clubs often refer to their weekly meeting as 'church'. In its purest form, for them the bond and the community they share together is relational. They may meet in a semi-fortified clubhouse, but the club is not the clubhouse, it's the members who are wearing the patch, and it's the fire in their belly for what they believe in that keeps them together.

Occasionally it goes wrong. People get out of hand, motives get sidetracked. Clubs fall out and people get hurt. Motorcycle clubs, like the Church, are made up of ordinary people. During a preliminary period, a new hopeful wanting to be a member of a club will be invited to initially 'prospect' – to begin to enter into the journey of club life. He will be pushed to the limits, tested to see if he is reliable, trustworthy and honourable enough to wear the club's colours.

On one occasion a small group of us, later to become the beginnings of God's Squad in the UK, were at a bike event. There was me, full of enthusiasm, sometimes too much for my own good, and the ever-present Spike, with whom I'd been in CMA leadership. His sometimes anarchistic tendencies and always very creative thinking made team-building a challenge, but he had a great knack of seeing through the fog when it came to problem-solving, and no matter how difficult the challenge, Spike would turn up to face it. An enormous young guy called Howie had recently got involved, and he would prove to be one of my most significant travelling companions over the next 20 years; his highly driven, extrovert, magnetic personality built relationships easily in clubhouses. Then there was Dave, who hardly said a word, but when he did you knew you needed to listen. His calm, quiet reassuring presence brought a measured stability in our formative days on the road. There was Psycho, who wasn't anything like his nickname would suggest – a gentle soul whose integrity, fortitude and steely faith would prove to be an essential backbone for the club as we grew and developed. And there was Soldier Steve who was, indeed, a soldier. He was a methodical, regimented, well-organized man who made sure we got things done and done as well as we possibly could, which given the diverse mix was often a challenge. Each man very different, each man not ideally suited, all with weaknesses, but each motivated by a faith in Christ to step beyond the walls of our churches and prepared to go out on the road together.

We were minding our own business, watching a band, when we became aware of a violent disturbance behind us. It resembled a scene in a saloon bar in the Wild West, while the band played on. Bodies and furniture were flying everywhere, and in the middle of it some prospects were attacking a couple of guys and beating them to a pulp. It was becoming very ugly, very quickly. I have no idea what the story was – maybe just a regular drunken bar brawl, or perhaps the prospects had taken offence and were defending their honour – but it turned into a nasty incident.

When there was a brief lull in the proceedings, as the injured lay semi-conscious amid a circle of adrenalin-filled aggressors, the group of us, without so much as looking at each other, moved forward as one unit, breaking into the circle and dragging the two bleeding and battered men out. They needed urgent medical attention. I didn't dare make eye contact with anyone in case we were going to be joining them, but I could feel everyone staring at us. We got them out of the venue, into a security van and to a medical centre. We looked a right sight, covered in their blood, so there was no chance of fading into the background.

The following morning we got word that our actions had gained the respect of many who had witnessed it. This incident proved an important point to me about the group of us who were wanting to be part of God's Squad. We were all moved to respond in the same way when the situation required it. It's all very well feeling called to a ministry on the margins, but sooner or later it will take some guts to step out with faith. Whatever we lacked in formal labelling at this time, we were beginning to function as a unit and that felt cohesive. We started riding as a group, we started thinking as a group. Most of our contact with clubs was at public events, but even in these days clubhouse invitations were coming our way and significant personal friendships had already developed with senior officers in some clubs.

These individual friendships proved crucial in brokering our desire to put up God's Squad colours. While God's Squad in Melbourne had long-established relationships with many clubs there, including some international ones, we had to earn our own right to speak and build our own credibility. Starting an intentional missional move within a subculture such as the motorcycle club scene would be a long process. Unless you want to risk upsetting everyone, which is what some Christian clubs have done, you need to play by the same rules. Becoming accepted to a certain degree before you start formally is par for the course. Putting in the miles, the time and the hard yards is what is expected.

God's Squad takes on the shape and structure of colours-wearing motorcycle clubs, but we put our own unique, Christ-influenced meaning to the processes and symbols. We wear colours on our backs and while our faith is a gift of God's grace, our colours are earned, not bought. They mark the culmination of a discernment process, but it's no easy ride getting into God's Squad. Typically it will take three to four years – not too different from many other back-patch clubs, and interestingly not too dissimilar to the length of time it takes to be ordained as a priest or accepted into a monastic order. We function with the same sort of structure of office bearers as other motorcycle clubs, with a clearly defined structure of leadership, discipline and accountability. The club is organized into regional chapters, and each member, prospective member and associate contributes financially to the running of the club. There are non-negotiables that define who we are, some of which stand in direct opposition to the subculture we are part of because our first allegiance is to the cause of Christ. Knowing when to make that stand requires tact, wisdom and a resolute resolve that won't buckle under pressure. It's a community of ministry that doesn't suit everyone. Eventually it requires something more than simply being a Christian and riding a motorcycle – an assurance of a radical call to mission, a commitment to be counter-cultural when necessary, and a willingness to function in a team of people just as dysfunctional as yourself. There may be uniformity in our colours, but there is a wildly eclectic mix of characters that make up the membership of God's Squad.

Setting up a new chapter of a club so far from the parent chapter in Melbourne was a little strange, especially in the beginning. As prospective members, partial colours are granted. The basic labelling consists of a curved arc, called a 'rocker', stating the club's geographical location, in our case 'United Kingdom', and 'CMC' standing for Christian Motorcycle Club, but without the central God's Squad insignia. This indicated that we were prospects, although it wasn't obvious who we were prospecting for as there were no other fully patched God's Squad members in the UK. But we had done some groundwork to make sure other clubs knew exactly who we were. Through our network of established contacts, we already had good relationships with key members in some clubs, and were able to inform many of the English clubs of our intentions to begin. The full club colours, our insignia, would be granted on completion of a suitable prospect period.

The responses we received were as expected, and generally one of three. 'Carry on, lads, we've no problem. Best of luck to you', 'We don't care', or 'Don't even think about it – if we see you, we'll rip your patches.' Being stripped of your club colours, whether they are removed in a disciplinary action within your own club or taken by force by another club, is a humiliation to be avoided. As was pointed out to me by one club member some years later, after I'd got punched and thrown out of an event, 'You can't please everyone all the time.' While this was certainly the case and always will be, we did what we could to gain the acceptance of as many as possible at the beginning. But it still took a step of faith and we regularly ran the gauntlet in places where a warm welcome was not guaranteed. As I reflect back, naivety must have played a part, but there was always a sincere sense that we were where God was calling us to be, and we were responding to that call. There was much that put us on edge and could have put us off early on, but also enough encouragement from within the scene to stick with it and see it through.

In the summer of 1994 the small group wanting to join God's Squad met with John Smith, who was once again in the UK for Greenbelt. He came with us to a major biker event. Hosted by one of the larger clubs, it had started some years before on a small scale, but now attracted in the region of 30,000 bikers. I had attended for several years along with Spike and a few others with missional intentions. It was a great event for John to experience and also to see how we functioned together and the relationships we had managed to build at this particular gathering. John and Woody, another Melbourne member and musician, were received well and very quickly saw the depth of relationship we had developed not only with clubs but with traders, magazine staff and the wider biking community generally.

The following day, feeling a little jaded after a late night, Jayne and I travelled with John and Woody down to London. John was due to preach at All Souls, Langham Place. This typifies Smith: hanging out with a bunch of bikers until the early hours of the morning, then a 120-mile journey to speak in one of the most famous pulpits in London. As John was giving his introduction, he mentioned the biking event he'd been to and commented that it looked likely there would be a chapter of God's Squad starting in the UK before too long. I'm sure due process wasn't followed at that point, but Woody elbowed me in the ribs and whispered, 'Looks like you're in!' I was delighted. We were the last to leave the church that night as we waited for John who, true to form, talked at length with every single person who wanted to bend his ear. The journey back up to the Midlands was a tiring one, but very satisfying.

Shortly after this, Spike, Dave and Howie and I began to prospect for God's Squad Christian Motorcycle Club. Psycho, Soldier and a few others were thinking about getting involved too, but felt they wanted more time. There was no turning back now. We were labelled as the first UK prospective members of God's Squad Christian Motorcycle Club and it was official. We thought we knew everything, but in reality we knew just about enough to make it.

Twelve months after John had been with us, he returned again to speak at Greenbelt and attended the same biker event. In summer 1995, five years after the first steps of initiating contact with him and God's Squad, four of us were granted membership by God's Squad in Melbourne, and we had the privilege of being presented with our God's Squad colours. The preceding year of prospecting had seen us put in a lot of miles, getting around as many clubs as we had contacts with. Sometimes we travelled huge distances in appalling weather with only a slight hope of bumping into people we wanted to meet. But early encounters also brought encouragement.

I remember well one club member telling me that after he had left a career in the army, disillusioned with his experience he considered investigating the Christian faith. He wanted a Bible and thought the best place to obtain one would probably be a church. He went along with the best of intentions, willing to pay for one if necessary. No one spoke to him, no one welcomed him; feeling rejected, he walked out of the church and dismissed the Christian faith. Several years later, and having found acceptance in a motorcycle club instead of the church, he welcomed us into his clubhouse. He began to appreciate that maybe God hadn't forgotten him after all. A long, cold ride in the rain becomes worthwhile when it can help rebuild a bridge.

God's Squad continues its tradition of being a club that's on the road. Although we put our own slant on the prospecting process compared to other clubs, there remains common ground. The probationary period is when things are learned, characters tested, relationships built and trust earned. It's important not just for the internal structure of our own club for this process to be obvious, but also for those clubs watching on. The one sure way for your colours, and therefore your club, not to be taken seriously is if they have not been earned, and patches are effectively given away cheaply.

This is one reason why the process of becoming a member of God's Squad continues to take three to four years. There are plenty of other reasons why the process is a lengthy one. It's the same for new members now as it was in the early days in the 1970s. You need to know who you have got on the road with you. Can you trust them? What does their faith in Christ really mean to them? Is this a ministry they are called to or an ego to be massaged? Have they got their life in balance? Can they juggle family, work and club commitments?

This isn't primarily a book about the development of God's Squad into Europe, but it remains an important part of my life and ministry. It is significant not just because of its surprising effectiveness considering our diverse collection of members, but because it's where I have found my place. A group of people took a risk with me and gave me a chance to run with what I was carrying in my heart. We should never underestimate the significance of finding where we belong. To the outsider looking in, it wasn't an obvious fit, though. The somewhat shy and introverted squeaky-clean son of a preacher finds his place and parish in a subculture that has a reputation for stamping out the first signs of weakness and is more likely to resemble the Wild West than any church.

My first Harley Davidson project in progress prior to completion.
A 1980 Ironhead Sportster engine in a 1962 rigid frame

The original group in 1994 that became the foundation of God's Squad
in the UK, back row: Howie, John Smith (Melbourne), Dave, Soldier,
Psycho; front row: Woody (Melbourne), Spike, Sean, Colin

The four original members of God's Squad CMC United Kingdom, 1995:
L.-R. Howie, Dave, Spike and Sean

United in mission, New South Wales, Australia, 2011

God's Squad CMC United Kingdom chapter, 2007, left to right:
Glenn (2004 to present), Matt (2006 to present), Nige (2005–10),
Baz (2007–12 GBNF), Tony (1999–2012), Psycho (1996 to present),
Tez (2000 to present), Soldier (1997–2008), Nick (2002 to present),
Howie (1995 to present), Sean (1995 to present), Martin (2006 to present)

My original 1995 colours,
'marinated in life on the road'

Is anyone listening? Occasionally
there are still voices crying in the
wilderness, 'Pete'

God's Squad now has chapters throughout Europe. Ukraine has been a place of personal challenge and transformation

Lloyds glass and Zac's Place – making something beautiful out of broken pieces

A distressed Jesus at Zac's Place. Remembering Andy, pondering Gethsemane

The flood plain at Gundagai in New South Wales, Australia, which inspired research for a remarkable story, 2009

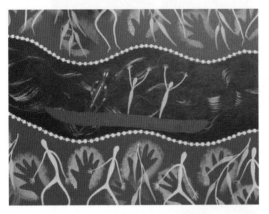

Blessed are the peacemakers. An excerpt from Yidinji's painting, reflecting on the Murrumbidgee river flood of 1852 and the heroic efforts of two local men

Reflecting in silence at the grave of 12-year-old Tarore, near Matamata, Aotearoa, 2013

Blessed are those who mourn, for they will be comforted.
The captivating life-size sculpture, affectionately called
'Doris', who is part of the Zac's Place Beatitudes
commission

Christmas day at Zac's Place in 2007 with Bob, who saw
what many others were missing on Wind Street

On the road with fellow God's Squad CMC South Wales member, Martin, 2010

My wheels, a modified 1999 FXDX, on the road with our God's Squad Pilgrim chapter in Ireland

Friendships formed on the road are some of the best. A pit stop with South Wales members Ric, Matt and Martin, and John from Ireland (front left), 2018

In full flight at Swansea Grand theatre at a fundraising gig, 2016

Don't let the light go out

8

Standing for something

You need an occasion that makes you feel like packing in the whole thing before you really test whether you have got what it takes for the long haul. The early years on the road with God's Squad were often uncertain times. While we had trusted friendships with some individuals and clubs, our existence wasn't universally celebrated.

Early on, we found ourselves at an event where there were a couple of club chapters we weren't very familiar with. It had been a constructive weekend, a long ride in good weather and we'd set up camp along with everyone else. The custom bike show, live music and beer tent were in full swing late into the night. Then, as things wound down, we found ourselves caught up in a discussion with several motorcycle club members who were aggrieved by our very presence. Before long we were encircled by a group of guys who were pumped up with alcohol and probably other preferred substances of choice. What started out as a bit of prodding and goading along the lines of 'Who the f— do you lot think you are?' soon became a full-on attack on the evils of the Church, highlighting historical cases of child abuse by priests. News headlines that week had brought these ugly and traumatic issues to the fore, and in the absence of any guilty priests, we had become the object of their wrath instead.

Very quickly, the scenario turned nasty. The subsequent physical onslaught prevents me from remembering too many details. What I do recall before the three of us hit the deck was the humiliating tirade of verbal abuse that preceded the physical beating. 'You guys are all the same, you Christians, I bet you're all like those pervert priests.' It continued as a group of women walked past: 'Come on, girls, these guys want to f— the devil out of you.' I remember thinking, 'Hope the first punch knocks me out.' As it turned out it was the second one. The first one was just a taster to see if we would fight back, but it's just never been in my locker and more to the point, I have never thought of Christ as a scrapper in that sense. Besides, beneath the aggression fuelled by alcohol there was a justified anger, if somewhat misdirected towards us, at the unjustifiable, sick actions of some priests. Maybe this news story had touched a raw nerve and brought pain to the surface and this had contributed to the aggressive response. The legacy and damage of sexual abuse permeates so much of our society and the bike scene is no exception; victims sometimes seek security in a closed band of brothers.

The following day the three of us, looking rather sorry for ourselves and nursing a collection of black eyes, fat lips, broken bones, busted teeth, cuts and bruises, cautiously exited the site and rode the long journey back to our respective homes. It has to be said that we didn't look like your average bunch of good churchgoing folk on their way home from chapel at this point! If ever there was a day to pack it all in, that could have been it. It was humiliating, it was painful and it cast doubts on whether this was a good idea. It was also deeply concerning for our loved ones when we got home – by this time we had young families. We always knew there would be risks, so was it worth it? What's more, I didn't like the thought of having enemies; loving your enemies all of a sudden got real.

A couple of things happened shortly after this. Within a day I received a call from someone associated with the men who had confronted us. He assured me that the matter would be dealt with, and nothing more was said about it. There are often hot-headed members around, but we have sometimes been able to nurture fruitful relationships with the more diplomatic members of the scene: the guys who have a respect for the stand we take, even though they may not embrace what we believe.

Back in the 1980s I remember seeing an *Arena* TV documentary about the famous Sturgis motorcycle gathering in South Dakota, USA. The programme included a feature about a national club who were attending the event. There were many stereotypical anecdotes, but also some fascinating candid moments. I recall a member of the club, who was also a devout Christian and their chaplain, saying of his brothers in the club, 'I don't always like what they do, but I understand what they believe', while of him, the club observed, 'They don't understand what he believes but they like what he does.' On that basis, he found grounds to have a functioning relationship with them. I think that sentiment covers it well for God's Squad too, and it would be a fair representative opinion as to where we fit.

While we have never been just available as chaplains to one club, or pledged any kind of allegiance to one other club, we have tried to respond as needed to any club that accepts and respects what we bring to the subculture. That political impartiality, with an allegiance to Christ, is an essential part of what our colours stand for and it emphasizes our motives of genuine love and care for our mates, a desire not to take sides in a political alliance or for kudos of association. That respect has been hard to earn and the fall-out from this beating was one of the most significant learning experiences.

Not long afterwards we received an invitation to a clubhouse gathering for a significant club anniversary party. We knew that the host club were likely to welcome us gladly but we had a good idea that the aggressors from the bike show would be in attendance as well. We could easily have made our excuses: the event meant a long ride in bad weather. But this was an opportunity to demonstrate that although we don't respond with physical violence and revenge, we have other ways of refusing to back down and demonstrating some steel.

Simply being willing to turn up in a closed, invitee-only environment and risk facing the same perpetrators in close proximity could make or break us. We chose to go. We walked into the venue and straight out in front of a stage where a blues band was playing. A couple of hundred guys were there drinking and very quickly I recognized the shapes of those who had administered the beating. As we kept walking into the crowd, a solitary figure came out of the shadows and embraced me. He was a senior officer of the host club and was making sure that everyone knew we were welcome, whether they were comfortable with that or not. I interpreted this as a huge statement on the part of him and his club, acknowledging the stand we made by being prepared to turn up and face the music. We could have opted out but we chose not to, and I know we gained a lot of respect from guys who weren't necessarily interested in what we believed at that stage. They just recognized that we had the guts to show up.

The small amounts of violence present in the biker subculture are more than balanced by the basic values that are both admirable and prevalent at its core. Sticking to what you believe and making a stand for it earns respect and wins friends eventually. No one would have blamed us if we had packed it all in having experienced violent opposition. In fact, various friends within other Christian biker circles thought we were making a huge mistake starting God's Squad in the UK. But we believed the Lord had called us to do this. This community deserved an opportunity to see a genuine expression of the Christian faith in its midst, that was there to love them and not condemn them. We just had to stick around long enough to earn respect in order to have a voice and any sort of influence.

As my bruises had faded from this beating, I attended a conference for preachers in Britain. While the on-the-road ministry with God's Squad was becoming established, I was still engaged in public speaking in churches, youth events and also ministry in various prisons. I maintained and nurtured networks and friendships in more traditional church circles. One of the keynote speakers at the conference commented that in the UK we don't really experience much opposition to our faith; just moments earlier, he and others had rather patronizingly said to me in passing, 'Well done, sonny, you're doing a good job', having no idea about the beating we had just taken, which was in no small part due to systemic failure of the wider Church. Sometimes the Church has been its own opposition in terms of both its blindness to its failures and its inability to interpret cultural contexts.

Meanwhile, on the road with God's Squad, other important milestones were achieved. We were called on to take or be involved with funerals, which were important occasions. Funerals are often times of a sincere deepening of relationships as we walk with the bereaved through dark days. In the motorcycle club scene they are huge occasions for the tribe to gather together. It's not uncommon for up to 1,000 bikers to attend funerals; allied clubs, friends and supporters travel from far and wide to pay their respects. The club's headquarters will take on a sombre tone in the days before the funeral. The dead brother will effectively be lying in state, his body in an open coffin in the clubhouse, perhaps in a specially curtained-off area where the club family can share their private moments. It is always dignified and respectful. Non-club members are also welcome to pay their respects, but often only in the company of a member.

At the bar in the clubhouse, stories will be shared over drinks all night as the rumble of Harleys arriving from far and wide punctuates the conversation. There will be warm embraces, reunions, and in a quiet corner club officers making sure the logistics are in place for giving their brother a respectful send-off the following day. By the time the cortege leaves the following morning, the neighbouring streets will be full of bikers. The coffin is carried on the shoulders of club brothers out to the hearse or other vehicle of choice – a sidecar, a trailer, a truck. In a regimented fashion, the club and guests organize themselves in strict formation and riding order behind the hearse, with the host club at the front. Once the cortege starts rolling, nothing will stop it. This unifying act of respect processes through town to the burial site. Different clubs have different traditions, the coffin sometimes being passed along giving each person an opportunity to share in carrying it. At the conclusion of a ceremony that may or may not involve religious content, once the coffin is placed in the ground the club brothers usually take shovels and fill the grave themselves.

Sometimes we were asked just to take part. Early on there was one funeral where the club wanted a humanist service, but the sister of the club member who had died wanted a psalm and the 'Footprints' poem read. The club didn't want to do it, the humanist celebrant wouldn't, so they asked us. That simple act deepened an already established relationship with the club to such an extent that they have called on our support several times since then to help them walk through their grief together and bring whatever we see fit of our Christian faith to the table.

In fact, the turnaround is quite remarkable. Fifteen years before this I was considered persona non grata, yet among the same community an officer now admitted, 'We may not believe the same as you, but we really need you guys around at these times.' It is hard to capture those sentiments; I wish I could bottle it and show you, because to gain the trust and respect of a subculture and be given a voice and an opportunity to serve does not come easily or cheaply. It probably took about ten years for me to appreciate that we were beginning to have some kind of impact. When a subculture gathers together and invites you to lead them through their darkest days because they value what you bring in your spirit, you know that despite all the setbacks, insults, beatings and misunderstandings, it's worthwhile because it makes a difference. Of course, in between these formal pastoral roles we take up invitations to attend clubhouse parties and enjoy deep friendships in many contexts. This is where the nitty-gritty of everyday life, faith, doubts and fears is worked out in the company of friends.

Funerals carry a significant amount of responsibility in tragic circumstances. Sometimes that is intensified when the circumstances are highly charged with emotion. Members of two particular clubs had been in conflict and men tragically died as a result. As is not uncommon for God's Squad, we were in relationship with all parties involved, so we had to make clear that by taking the funeral we weren't choosing one side over the other in their ongoing conflict. This neutrality was understood and we also committed ourselves not only to walk alongside the grieving but to try to be an influence for peace. We certainly prayed hard and were in a position to talk to various individuals. Whether or not we had any influence I really do not know, but I am thankful that I have not had to take too many funerals in such circumstances. In the UK at least, extreme violence between motorcycle clubs is relatively rare.

We continue to try to be advocates for wise choices and peace in a subculture that can be fuelled by male egos. Some governments sell the idea that all motorcycle clubs are criminal gangs whose only agenda is organized crime. After 25 years of personal pastoral support among many of these clubs around the world, I know that simply isn't true.

Sometimes blokes just need to belong to a tribe. The bike scene is one of the few areas of Western society where the tribal culture still functions. One premise of the brotherhood is that although there is a structure, everyone is equal and has a role. Therefore, if the club were to exist solely for the purposes of organized crime, then the whole club would benefit equally from its proceeds. However, I know from experience, having visited guys in these clubs in their own homes, that some live in great wealth while others in the same chapter are living in bedsits and struggling to keep a bike on the road. If there are proceeds from organized crime kicking around, then the distribution of it doesn't appear to be well organized at all. Of course, there may be individuals involved in criminal activities in some clubs and maybe the odd rogue chapter, but you cannot make a sweeping generalization about a whole global subculture, demonizing those who associate with the individuals concerned. If you put a magnifying glass on any sector of society you will find dishonesty and some level of crime. Motorcycle clubs may have their criminal elements, in some countries more than others, but that is not in my experience the primary attraction for belonging.

The formative years of God's Squad in the UK continued to be a challenge, but gradually we became more accepted in a chaplaincy and priestly role among a greater number of clubs than we ever thought possible. There will always be some places we are not entirely welcome, and some find our neutral stance with regard to inter-club politics unacceptable, but we have chosen to acknowledge that this is one of the non-negotiables about what our colours stand for; to compromise this would be to compromise what we are at the core – followers of Christ first.

Sometimes my own stubborn enthusiasm has nearly landed me in trouble, though. On one occasion I turned up at a clubhouse unannounced, determined to find my way without phoning for directions. As the Harley rumbled through the urban environment, the deep exhaust note bounced off the steel cladding of industrial buildings. On hearing the unmistakable tone, an eagle-eyed member in the clubhouse mistook me for a biker he had a significant grievance with, and proceeded to take aim with a shotgun. It was only with the quick thinking of another member who took a wild guess it was me that the gun was withdrawn just in time. I was blissfully unaware of this, and only enlightened considerably later how close I was to having a chest full of lead. It remains, I shall assume, an isolated incident but serves as a reminder that a surprise visit, no matter how well intended, may not always be welcome.

There are many precious stories collected along the road with God's Squad over the years. Even within our own ranks we have men who have come to faith during the years we have been on the road and who now follow Christ wearing the colours of God's Squad. We continue to be an oddball mix of men. As a senior officer of the club, I'll often be leading the pack of bikes on a club run and it never ceases to amaze me as I look in the rear-view mirror and recount the stories of the guys I see riding in formation behind me. None more so than Spen.

The day I received my God's Squad colours I literally bumped into Spen in a beer tent at a large event. He'd been drinking all day and was there with his club, of which he was Sergeant at Arms, meaning he was responsible for discipline. He looked at me, span me round and read my new set of patches. 'God's Squad? What the f— is that all about?' Spen's story is long, complex and painful and one that he chooses to keep mostly private. But at its heart is a tender tale of transformation that has surprised even some of his most long-standing his friends.

Seventeen years on from that first encounter and after many lengthy discussions at clubhouses and bars, Spen, having parted from his old club due to his destructive pattern of behaviour, eventually found faith in Christ. First he had to reach a point, however, that by his own admission was one stop short of a coffin to give him reason to change. The heartache that he has worked through with the pastoral support of Howie, a fellow founding UK member, has been a long but liberating process and he eventually joined God's Squad with his old club's blessing.

We set out to influence a subculture, and looking back I know that the attitude of our friends in so many clubs towards Christ and the Church is very different from what it was 20 years ago because of the deep friendships we have formed with mutual trust and respect. For some individuals it has brought radical personal transformation by allowing the sweet Spirit of Jesus to fix the bits that are busted and broken. Spen is one of those, who is now quite at home looking you in the eye and saying, 'I love you, brother', and knowing what that means. His face tells a thousand stories of pain, questions, mistakes and excesses. But his eyes now tell a story of transforming grace illuminating a soul that is at peace with himself, the world he lives in and his God.

I think too of John, a muscular, angry, former special forces soldier in an Irish club, in which he held a senior position. I didn't know his name at the time, or much of his story, but while we were taking up the invitation of a club to their weekend party, John saw us leaving the beer tent and main stage area just as the strippers were about to perform to a crowd of lecherous drunk Irishmen. John remembers more than I do of the occasion, and apparently he took the opportunity to point out our departure and hurled a mouthful of intimidating abuse in my direction as we moved away from the stage area.

Some months later our paths crossed again. John was in a more reflective mood and we spoke at length on matters of life, family and faith as we warmed ourselves with some soup in the early hours of the morning. That was the last time I saw him for years. His life unravelled, but our conversation had challenged him about his priorities. He left the bike club scene, and eventually found faith in Christ and a peace that enabled him to deal with the chaos he had lived in. His story, along with that of two other former soldiers, is recorded in a book, *About Face.*[2] John went on to work alongside people with issues of substance abuse and became passionate in his commitment of faith. Many years after I was on the receiving end of that tirade of cocaine-induced verbal abuse, John has become a friend and brother in the ministry of God's Squad, out on the road, wearing the same colours. He has managed to make the transition back into the subculture that almost destroyed him, with a renewed foundation of love and faith serving as a beacon of hope to others.

Transitions like John's and Spen's back into the bike scene with a new-found faith are not necessarily easy. At our God's Squad Melbourne chapter clubhouse, I talked late into the night with a good friend and fellow life member. When God's Squad became established in the early 1970s in Melbourne, he was president of a Melbourne-based motorcycle patch club. He watched with interest the new young Christian upstarts find their feet. Were they a front for the police? Were they having a laugh? These were not just his questions, they were the questions of numerous other clubs at the time. Eventually, with whatever reservations he had about God's Squad, he saw enough to draw him towards a life committed to following Christ; within a few years he joined God's Squad and he has been a dedicated active member since.

He, like others, has made the transition back into the bike scene with his faith, but I was fascinated to discover that even after nearly four decades there was still a tension within him. The fine line between doing the right thing and being sucked back into old patterns of behaviour and attitudes remains a challenge. On the surface, you would never know that battle exists for him, and to his credit he has quietly walked the line of a disciplined, faithful life. Whenever we face difficulties, the temptation to return to previous patterns of behaviour is very real. This club brother continues to face this temptation every time he encounters an attitude in a clubhouse that could spark him off. Spen and John also know what it is like to take steps backwards as well as forward. It remains both a challenge and an honour to share those steps alongside these three men from three different countries, and many others like them.

Earning respect and gaining credibility takes time, and we can never assume that everyone understands or appreciates our role and position when we take a stand. At one club event, having just engaged in warm conversation with members of that club, in a bizarre twist I walked around the corner and was immediately confronted by another member who took great personal offence that we had engaged in pastoral support recently of a club he considered his enemy. Our neutrality was a matter of huge concern and I was dragged by the scruff of the neck and unceremoniously escorted off the site. This had significant implications, not least for our other members still on the site and those yet to arrive. Now outside the camp, I had concerns about my members and I had others contacting me wondering what on earth had happened. We were left with little alternative. If the President gets thrown off a site then the whole club leaves too, no question about it. My chapter members made a point of leaving as one unit, taking with it our support vehicle containing all the hospitality equipment we had planned to use among our various friends over the weekend.

We rode home in a tight pack, the thunder of a dozen or more Harley Davidsons on song. Martin's old shovelhead's electrics were failing and he ran without lights, tucked into the left protected by others on all sides. It was summer but we weren't expecting a night ride and fingers were numb. Bodies were full of adrenalin and minds were racing as to the potential fallout of this. We had worked so hard to build up relationships across many clubs, and this knock-back was a tough one to take. Was this an individual grievance or did it go much further? Pride was a little bruised. Ultimately as President I would take responsibility if I had been in the wrong, but the ride that night was far from divisive.

In fact it was unifying, cohesive and purposeful, as we all knew that there are some things God's Squad will not back down on, and one of those is our neutral stance when it comes to the inter-club politics of the bike scene. The moment we take sides, we show an allegiance greater than that to our Saviour and this is non-negotiable; to water this down would be a betrayal of what our colours stand for. Tom Petty's song

'I Won't Back Down' is a personal favourite of mine and an anthem within God's Squad. The lyric advocates a stubborn refusal to compromise what you believe in even when staring into hell itself. Sometimes it pays to stand your ground and not dilute your foundational principles. Twelve months later we were back at the same event, resurrected as guests, hosting a BBQ for several other clubs on the site, and I was invited to lead a wedding blessing on the main stage.

As I look in the bike mirror at those behind me I see transformed lives, but also that some faces have gone. It has not all been smooth going. For some, the realization that wearing a God's Squad patch requires more than a token Christian faith and a motorcycle becomes a stumbling block. For others, while their faith and calling is strong it's tough to be a team player for the long haul. Ours is a tribe that should be marked by servant leadership, but sometimes it goes wrong, personalities clash, grace is forgotten and people lose heart. The loss of some along the way can be heartbreaking.

One of our long-serving members in Melbourne, Australia, the Revd Dave Fuller, has often put forward the view that the fact God's Squad has lasted as long as it has and grown the way it has is ultimately a testimony to God's grace. In theory it shouldn't work; we are far too dysfunctional, diverse and chaotic. In practice it is not an unspoilt road trip in glorious sunshine, it has at times been a hard slog, marked with heartache and pain. But it has also been a journey of tender transformation, remarkable faith and fortitude and a staunch commitment to stand for what you believe in.

I sought to establish God's Squad Christian Motorcycle Club in the UK as a viable expression of Christian ministry in a subculture that was never going to throw its arms wide open to the church community. But amid the egos, bonds of brotherhood and codes of honour we have sought to make a difference. John Chrysostom, a fourth-century priest who held fast to the radical teachings of Christ against a backdrop of a

Church that was selling out as it became the official religion of Rome, reflected on the foolishness of trying to change the world with a simple message of love and peace. He concluded, 'Doesn't the crucifixion of Christ give us ample reason to be frightened? Yes; but his Resurrection gives us superhuman courage.'[3] As I reflect, it has been a journey punctuated by many valleys and peaks, there has been much to be intimidated by and much that might be considered foolish. But ultimately it has been a journey with Christ alongside the broken, and that remains a work of God's resurrection grace.

9

Broken spokes

————◆◆◆————

Having spent a few years in the East Midlands, Jayne and I took the decision to relocate to her home city of Swansea in South Wales. Swansea is a coastal university city with a population of around 250,000. It's a city that has a wonderful, passionate sense of identity and rich history in culture and industry. Sadly, much of the steel, copper and coal industry around which the city developed is long gone and it now ranks as one of the economically poorer cities in Britain. It was heavily bombed in the Second World War and hastily rebuilt, which is a great shame as its position on the Gower peninsular means that it is surrounded by some of the most spectacular coastline anywhere in the world. True Swansea 'Jacks' take great pride in their identity and there continues to be enormous rivalry, not just in sporting terms, with near neighbour Cardiff.

Like in other large, densely populated areas in Wales, the indigenous Welsh language is not spoken much in Swansea, although it is more common in rural communities. Having said that, in recent years there has been a resurgence of Welsh. I was very conscious of being an Englishman moving to a different country, and the history of the English anywhere on the road over the centuries has not always left a good legacy, Wales included. I failed English exams at school quite spectacularly, accompanied by abject failures in French and German. The chances of my learning Welsh were always going to be slim. As a small measure of making good, Jayne and I have ensured that all four of our children were educated entirely through the medium of Welsh and were bilingual from a very young age.

Waiting for us in Swansea were Jayne's family and her home church, which had been so supportive for many years. I had already made some solid connections with local bikers, but deep down I was wondering what on earth I was going to do in Swansea. For someone who was covering in the region of 25,000 miles a year on the bike, it seemed that Swansea was not the smartest place to move to. It wasn't quite the end of the line, but came pretty close. There had been no booming voice from heaven or writing on the wall this time confirming that this was where God might be leading us. For me it was more a quiet peace and the realization that it didn't matter where we were based; what was important was that we served God as a family wherever we were.

The reality was, I knew that much of my ministry would continue to be on the road. But ministry can become a cruel mistress, allowing pride and obsession to cloud judgements. Over the years I have too often seen children and families of ministers pay a price for the cause of ministry that in all honesty could have been avoided. As much as I believe God has called me to minister among my mates in the bike scene, among the misfits, the outcasts, the artists and the odd, I know he has called me to be the best husband and best father I can be.

I often get asked in a bike clubhouse, 'What's the most important thing in your life?' Most guys in motorcycle clubs will say it's their patch, their club. Christians may say that it's God, family, work, friends, in that order, or something similar. Over the years I have come to find a balance I am at peace with. I continue to take seriously the words of Christ, particularly in the Sermon on the Mount when he speaks of seeking God first and his righteousness. This speaks of an expectation of God to make basic provision for us in what we'll wear, and eat, and I would continue the train of thought to include matters of where we live, whom we marry, how we raise our children and how we use our time. So for me it's always about putting God first. It's about being available, open and willing to serve him, living under the Lordship of Christ. As we live in the light of this, in these moments of surrender if you like, I believe that God gives us wisdom to make wise choices.

There are always myriad competing and conflicting demands on time: when to be at home, when to be at work; times to be on the road, times to spend in exclusive intimacy, times for rest and reflection and times for letting your hair down and having fun. Sacrifices still need to be made, maybe when I need to be away or in our home when our space is shared by a friend in need. But as I have sought to put God first, I sincerely believe that this has helped me apportion my time. It may be simply not answering the phone when I am partway through reading the children a story or playing a game, or putting the demands of ministry on hold as we celebrate a family occasion. I have come to learn, with varying degrees of success and failure, that to truly live under the Lordship of Christ is not about a list of priorities. It is more about placing Christ at the centre of your turning world, finding a measure of balance in each spoke that fans out, carefully maintaining each of them.

On one occasion when riding across the Severn suspension bridge, spanning the estuary border between England and Wales, the whole back end of my bike collapsed without warning. I had a passenger, it was pouring with rain and the rear of the bike was snaking back and forth across all three lanes of the motorway. In those fleeting seconds I was convinced I was going to lose control. I gradually wrestled the bike to the hard shoulder and I and my passenger, Aussie Glenn, sat there in silence and utter disbelief that we had managed to stay upright. I had brief visions of our demise head first in the mud of the River Severn 40 metres below, had we hit the side and bounced over the barriers. Initially I thought the frame had fractured or the suspension collapsed, but it transpired that two spokes had snapped. We later found them inside the punctured inner tube.

Over the years I've seen too many people suffer catastrophic blowouts because they haven't paid attention to keeping the different aspects of their life in balance. It's usually the family that suffers one way or another, and suddenly life blows out because of a gradual ignoring of basic maintenance.

The move to the East Midlands allowed us to get God's Squad on the road. The move to Swansea was because it made sense for us as a family. While it didn't stop me asking what on earth I was going to do there, behind the question was a sense of peace that God was not far from us.

10

Emergence of Zac's Place

At this point, after about eight years of ministry, I was aware that there was a pattern of behaviour I was becoming increasingly uncomfortable with. In various parts of the country guys within the bike scene and sometimes their families were coming to faith in Christ. Conversions were real and there was a genuine sense of transformation and desire to follow Christ. But there was a repeating pattern of frustration.

Despite an obvious work of God's grace in people's lives it was a constant battle for many of these folk to become settled in a local church community. This wasn't just a biker thing – I was aware of it in relation to other fringe groups too. I am well versed in understanding the language and images of most mainstream church denominations, but it is a completely alien environment for those who have not grown up with it, whatever flavour you happen to choose. If you were to reverse the roles, it would be like asking your average churchgoer to step inside the local bikers' clubhouse. A mixture of fear and discomfort would prevail. The church experience reminded some of them of school assemblies or going to court, as everyone sat in rows, facing the speaker at the front. For others the language just didn't make sense, and some felt ignored, patronized or judged – treated like a freak show or put on a pedestal because they had an interesting story to tell. And in reality, that's how they were made to feel: that they didn't belong. Bear in mind that this wasn't the experience in just one denomination, it was across the board. Some felt that their pastoral issues were too complex, or that it was all about the ego of the leadership;

some found the whole experience rather bland, with repeated attempts to be hip and cool adding to the frustration. In all honesty, I often found myself in complete agreement with these reasons, but felt powerless to do anything, not least because I was often somewhat removed geographically from them.

I had foolishly thought that those young in the faith would be nurtured and able to grow once initial introductions were made. But gradually, more often than not, people drifted away. Something wasn't connecting and it weighed heavy on my heart that here were people who genuinely wanted to follow Christ but their efforts to find a Christian community in a local context were falling flat time after time. It was heartbreaking. At the time we moved to Swansea I made a promise to myself that this had to change. If I was going to be engaged in helping people to discover faith in Christ, then I had to be involved for the long term in their discipleship and nurturing their faith. If the organized church wasn't ready for them, or prepared to change the shape of their mould, then maybe we would just have to meet the need and create a 'disorganized' church.

I had been batting the idea around of some kind of church gathering in a pub for a while before we moved. This included chatting with Lorraine, a good friend of Jayne's who was a singer-songwriter. She was facing similar issues with a lot of her musician friends: they were comfortable talking about matters of faith in the recording studio but there was no way they were going anywhere near a church. Sometime before, back in Reading, I had a bikers' tribal gathering going at Ben Spiller's house, which had hosted many events over the years. A few bikers began to gather for Bible study and encouragement, travelling from around a 50-mile radius. Prior to that, I also experimented with a gathering at a mate's house in a different part of Reading.

Phil was a close mate. We had met when he was at Yeldall Manor drug rehab several years before. I used to meet the lads there once a week for a game of football and more recently

Phil and I had worked together on a mission team at my home church in Reading. Phil had been clean of drugs for several years but had a setback while we were working together. He disappeared during a conference that was particularly tedious and in hindsight quite offensive in its theological approach to matters of struggle and hardship. He relapsed and never really fully recovered. Tragically he died from an accidental overdose a few years later. But during this period his faith was tangible and his questions were real and deserved answers. We were talking about the story of Zacchaeus in Luke's Gospel, how Jesus voluntarily chose to spend time with this outcast despite the scornful response from religious onlookers. Jesus ends up at his house, eating, sharing stories – and ultimately Zac has a complete transformation of his character and behaviour. We liked that.

The story particularly resonated with me because Zac was significantly small in stature. Maybe he turned to the dark side and worked for the Romans to extort every penny he could from his Jewish neighbours because this was his way of getting even for the ribbing he took for being short. We liked that Jesus went to his place knowing that it would be an unpopular choice with the locals.

We thought that 'Zac's Place' would be a great name for a church community – where Jesus hangs out. That was in 1995, and Phil died shortly after. It was heartbreaking, but the seeds of our discussion stayed with me and I am convinced that if Phil were alive still he would have moved to Swansea and got involved with what Zac's Place grew into.

Other small experimental one-off gatherings took place. A small retreat on Gower on a wet and stormy summer weekend became an opportunity for about a dozen invited friends who were struggling at the time to make sense of church to gather, share stories and encourage each other. Late on the Saturday night we gathered around a fire overlooking the beach and shared communion together. This was a cohesive time, until I passed Len the bottle of 'sacramental' red wine. Len had come to faith quite recently through our Bibles for Bikers project. He had been dry for years, not a drop of alcohol had passed his lips; it had been vital for him to keep on top of the alcoholism that had caused so much damage in his earlier life. I shall never forget his expression, nor he mine, and in a moment of panic I hastily grabbed a bottle of diet cola as a replacement. Even the smallest things can be the biggest of stumbling blocks. To this day, if I am given a choice between alcoholic and non-alcoholic sacramental wine, I will usually choose non-alcoholic, as a symbolic act of solidarity standing with my many friends who continue to battle with alcohol addiction and recovery.

This gathering happened in the summer of 1998. We had been in Swansea for about 18 months and it was now ten years since my home church in Reading first commissioned me into mission on the margins. I was a solitary God's Squad member in the area, as were the other five members in the Midlands, Manchester, Bath, Hampshire and Oxfordshire. We functioned on the road together, but also got on with making contacts on our own doorstep.

I was asked to take the funeral of a popular local biker in Swansea, which I did willingly. I had already got to know many in the community but this cemented the relationships. None of us was aware then that just a few weeks later we would all be back at the same crematorium saying goodbye to another brother who tragically died in an accident. The whole local biking community was in shock and many were asking some big questions of faith and life. Responses to my words at both services were very warm and respectful and led to numerous people asking if they could come and talk more, but there was no way they were going to go near what they understood to be a church. I continued to do what I could to comfort the bereaved, while weighing up whether this was a good time to revisit the idea of some sort of church gathering in a public bar.

I co-opted Lorraine and sought the support of a few local clergy. We expected some kind of backlash from a predominantly teetotal church culture, so having a few supportive church leaders would to be important. I remain immensely thankful to Alistair Hornal and Dave Cave for their early support. Alistair I knew from Reading; he had moved to Mount Pleasant Church in Swansea just after us. Dave Cave arrived in Swansea just before us, coming from a church in Liverpool where I had met him some years before while on tour with John Smith. I had a long list of what I knew we didn't want and a very small list of things we did want to include as part of the framework for what became 'Zac's Place – Church in a Pub?' The question mark was always important. To be honest, we really didn't know if Zac's Place would be a church, or would grow into being a church community, or would be just a short series of gatherings that would fizzle out after a few weeks. We had absolutely no idea.

The more I have explored what it is to be part of the church community, the more it seems to be about relationships. There is something of a barrier built between a lectern or an altar and a congregation. The 'us and them' feeling invites participation from a select few, and before long a community of people become spectators of a performance. This can be applied equally across many denominations. Our fascination in the West with giving prominence to extrovert personalities in leadership doesn't just apply to corporations and governments. It has crept into the Church, particularly in nonconformist denominations where personality rather than substance can become a dominating feature, where symbols and sacred acts no longer point to Christ but to personalities instead. So much of what we assert as being biblical for the way we 'do church' is open to question.

Before the time of the Emperor Constantine there were no church buildings, no professional clergy and no 'Sunday church' as many of us experience it or imagine it. For its first few hundred years the Christian Church gathered in homes, around tables, sharing food, sharing possessions and committed to following Jesus, often against a backdrop of intense persecution as they flew in the face of popular opinion and behaviour. The reality is that what many of us experience as church has been shaped enormously by factors other than Christ. Whether it be the Roman basilica or the glitzy 'God bless America' corporate wonder show, popular culture has influenced the Church. While we often need to be attentive to local culture and learn to speak the local language and communicate with relevant images, sadly large elements within the Church have been unhealthily influenced by pagan culture. Obviously we shouldn't shut ourselves away. The apostle Paul became an expert at cross-cultural dialogue, as his journeys took him to new places with traditions of paganism, mysticism and mythology, all a long way from his Jewish heritage.

But there is also a time to put the brakes on and ask some serious questions. How much of what we are doing as church is really about Christ and his glory? How much of what we are doing is about cultural habit, or putting on a performance to present an acceptable image? I continue to wrestle with these questions. I am writing these words in the solitude and silence of a Benedictine monastic community. In between bouts of writing, I share the Eucharist with a small number of monks and nuns for whom I have huge admiration and respect. In raising these questions I am not dismissing the significant value I see in many different expressions of Christian community, but I do want to challenge us to strip everything back to what is essential. What does it all hang on? What is the skeleton over which the fragile flesh of the Christian Church can form? Too often we take it as a given that this is the way it is and there is no alternative.

The reason I can be at home in a silent monastic community is because I enjoy being in the company of deeply committed people. At its most basic, that is what the church community should be – a gathering of deeply committed people, committed to the cause of Christ and the outworking of that in the lives of those they live with and share the wider community with. How we do that is not set in stone. In fact, Jesus left very few instructions on being church as we know it. The ones he did leave had connotations of a community of oddball believers rather than how to run an institution for the elite.

As I began to consider what it might mean to plant a church, I had already stripped everything right back to the bare bones. I love rock music and there's nothing I enjoy more than Bruce Springsteen's E Street Band in full swing with a horn section behind screaming guitars, a bass drum that punches you in the guts and a monster snare drum sound that explodes between your ears. But equally, if a song is a great song, it will stand up when it is stripped back with minimalist production and warm acoustic tones – producers like T Bone Burnett have done this with many artists in recent years and it's what Eric Clapton did with his groundbreaking 'unplugged' MTV session. I wonder whether church has become so overproduced and distorted that we can no longer hear the original melody or feel the intended natural rhythmic order amid the layers and loops of extras in the mix that may not be as essential as we might think.

I have found it helpful to ask three questions when considering any activity relating to church life, whether it be the place of the sermon, corporate worship, feeding the poor, running children's clubs or absolutely anything else. These were also the three questions I asked when we began the journey of Zac's Place. They all hinge on relationship.

- How does what we do affect the relationship we have with God?
- How does what we do affect the relationships we have with one another?
- How does what we do affect the relationship we have with the wider community?

If we cannot find a positive response to at least one of these questions, preferably all three, then in my mind it raises serious doubts as to whether the activity is wasting our time and resources.

With these thoughts forming in my mind, and joined by Lorraine and one or two others, we set about organizing our first Zac's Place gatherings in a Swansea bar. Off the list of priorities went corporate singing, sitting in rows and a long sermon. There was no point just dumping in a bar what went on in every other church setting – the only change would be in the ambience, which can make a difference but in the big scheme of things is peripheral. The idea of 'niche' church was never going to happen either. While we wanted bikers, musicians and artists to be at home and welcome, it had to be an open door to absolutely everyone. There are certain things that it is best to learn in peer groups, but I have never thought that such a narrow focus is healthy for church relationships. Jesus picked a diverse mix of disciples for a reason: they each brought something different to the table, they all had different perspectives and different issues to deal with.

It wasn't to be a 'meeting' with an agenda, but a gathering with relationships at the heart. While the sermon was out, the Bible certainly wasn't. We would make room for short biblical reflections that were easy to understand but did not compromise the meaning and go soft on content. Corporate singing as we knew it was out, but we did plan to use songs that told stories, and we wanted to capture people's imagination with creative music. Public prayer would be limited to a blessing at the end of the night, but a book would be available on the bar for people to write prayers and prayer requests in. There would be no surprises and no getting people in under false pretences. We weren't going to run a big advertising campaign, it was word of mouth. Those who needed to know were told about it.

We decided we would gather every week on a Sunday night. That made it easy to remember. Sundays were a quiet night in the pub trade back then, musicians weren't usually gigging and bikers were back home from a weekend on the road. It wasn't going to be about a stage, it was about people gathered around tables and a bar talking and sharing. Neither would it be a church that emerged from the disgruntled back row of existing churches; if it was emerging from anywhere it was from the street and our collective established mission field. We didn't try to seek the support of those we knew would oppose it and we didn't pretend it would be anything other than what it was – an attempt to respond to the questions of searching souls who felt that mainstream church was too alien.

In October 1998 we secured the Sunday night use of a basement bar in Swansea city centre; at the time it was called Subterranea. It was an old, dimly lit cellar with a curved ceiling and stone floors. Smoke lingered easily. It was a popular party and live music venue with a restaurant above. We mentioned it to friends and other people we thought would be interested. 'Zac's Place – Church in a Pub? Expression of and inquiry into the Christian faith in a relaxed environment' was how we described those early gatherings.

Would anyone come? We had absolutely no idea, but we need not have worried. Right from the start we had a couple of dozen people, some we knew, some we didn't. Most had very little connection with other aspects of church community. This was the beginning of an ongoing journey which in its first seven years included over 300 Sunday-night gatherings in four different bars.

A bar lends itself to being somewhere people can talk to each other – a social venue that thrives on social interaction. A pub where everyone sits in rows looking towards a single focal point makes the evening a performance. There's a limit to how well you can get to know anyone when you are staring at the back of their head. That is what has happened to the Church over the centuries – a far cry from groups gathering around meal tables in homes.

Sitting around tables or standing at the bar, people felt welcome and at ease. The interaction that happened around these tables was considered to be as important as what happened out at the front. I would introduce each gathering and explain who we were – Zac's Place, a church in pub, just in case anyone had just drifted in or been brought along by a well-meaning friend under false pretences. We'd have a couple of reflective songs, then I would offer a thought for the day and a bit later there'd be some more music. I would point out the notebook on the bar for prayers and prayer requests, and at the end there would be a blessing.

It wasn't rocket science, and that was appreciated. We were blessed not just with Lorraine's exceptional musical talents but with a plethora of wonderful songwriters who appeared out of the woodwork, many interestingly with their own struggles with church and faith. Songs that raised questions, expressed doubts and told heartfelt, honest stories of struggle, rebellion, fear, grief, faith and the hope of better days resonated in the hearts of those present. We certainly had bikers and musicians but we also attracted people from all walks of life and across the social spectrum.

I clearly remember one night when we gathered in the function room of a music venue called Ellington's above the Duke of York pub. It was Halloween and a busy night – maybe 60 or 70 people were in. It still makes me smile as I recall the bizarre mix of personalities that gathered around one of the tables. One of these was Phil the camper, puffing on a fat cigar and supping on a Guinness someone had bought him. Phil lived outside by the marina in a pile of rubbish and timber packing crates. In his mind, he was sailing the seven seas aboard his carefully crafted vessel. In reality, he wasn't going anywhere except walking to Neath every two weeks to pick up his pension.

Phil was a larger-than-life character and would frequent a few churches in the city. Most people groaned as he walked in because they knew he would launch into an abusive outburst if the preacher happened to mention a few key words, such as politics. His psychotic and muddled mind frequently got him into trouble, but we never had a problem with him. In fact, he had become a friend. Sometimes when riding back into Swansea in the small hours of the morning I would drop in to see him in his 'shanty ship' for a cuppa before getting home. He always appreciated that and somehow managed to translate it into showing us due respect at Zac's Place. Tragically, Phil was murdered for the price of a bottle of wine a few years after this, but he was an early part of our Zac's family and taught me a lot just by being himself.

Sitting near Phil was a visiting university professor from Ecuador. He was just passing through, here for a few months, and enjoyed the interaction. Close by was a television presenter and a former Page Three model with her husband, who just happened to be there because a friend of theirs was one of our regular musicians. You couldn't have made it up: from day one, our open-door policy has always delivered welcome surprises.

These formative years in the pubs were learning places for me too. I was used to communicating informally in clubhouses, so the environment wasn't unfamiliar. But I was used to preaching lengthy sermons from a pulpit, so keeping to a self-imposed time limit of five to ten minutes was a huge discipline. To take something of Christ and the Scriptures and encapsulate it successfully in a punchy, intelligible way that would stimulate ongoing discussion was a skill that needed to be honed. That apprenticeship has served me well; making every sentence count, especially when dealing with the media, for example, or even taking funerals, when you need to convey important sensual words in a very limited timeframe to people who will not just sit there and listen to nonsense. In the pub there was always room for questions, jovial heckling and banter. But behind it all was a sincere wish to make a connection with people and to convey something of the divine love of God to this ordinary diverse mix of searching souls.

There were two pubs we used as a base for about three years each. Ellington's I have already mentioned. It was here that some real momentum gathered. Word got around that it was a cool place to hang out on Sunday nights. We had worked in partnership with the secular television network HTV on a series of five programmes broadcast on ITV Wales on Sunday afternoons. Mal Pope, a local songwriter and broadcaster, hosted an established religious programming slot and the TV channel warmed to the idea of a run of programmes based around what we were doing in the bar. They wanted to call it *Zac's Place* – but I stuck to my guns and insisted that if they did that then they got me and the whole bunch of musicians and artists that make up who we are. After a lot of discussion, we went ahead with the filming on location in a bar in Swansea's marina. The Zac's Place programmes were fronted by Mal and included two live music acts, an interview and a short piece I wrote and presented to camera for each show. It was liberating to have the freedom to write my own material, and although I had plenty of previous television interview opportunities, the experience I had gained of having to keep it concise paid off. I'm still pleased with those short anecdotes, many years on.

It was a great experience on many levels and a catalyst for some special relationships. Favours were called in from old friends, including the ever supportive songwriter Martyn Joseph, whose captivating live performances express the hope and questions of the human soul so poignantly, and poet and broadcaster Stewart Henderson, who brought his linguistic genius with wit and candour. Comedians Tim Vine and John Archer, sax maestro Ben Castle and writer Adrian Plass also participated. I was delighted when a recent acquaintance, songwriter Rick Elias, flew in from Nashville to sing his song 'Man of No Reputation', a favourite of mine. Rick had recently been working with Tom Hanks on the film *That Thing You Do* and had also performed at World Youth Day at the Vatican in front of a couple of million people. To have him take the time to travel over not just for the TV filming but to play the smoky bar on the Sunday night was really special and it was an experience that brought him well and truly down to earth! A host of our regular Zac's Place performers earned their first TV appearances on the shows, including a very young Iain Hornal; he wrote the theme tune for the series and went on to become a respected songwriter. At the time of writing he is part of Jeff Lynne's ELO touring band. We were indeed surrounded by some wonderfully creative people.

One important relationship in the Zac's Place story also blossomed on the TV filming set. At the outset of the planning, Mal invited an old friend of his to be interviewed on the first programme. It was Rowan Williams, then Archbishop of Wales. Not knowing Rowan, my initial gut reaction was: what on earth do we want a stuffy Anglican bishop on the show for? It turned out to be a masterstroke on the part of Mal and producer Kate Miles. Rowan brought an air of establishment to what could be interpreted as a rather off-the-wall series of programmes. He also sent out a ringing endorsement for what we were trying to do with Zac's Place in the bigger picture away from these series of programmes.

Rowan and I got on very well. His far superior intellect was cushioned by a wonderful humility and a desire both to encourage us in what we were doing and to be open to learning from us too. At that time, he was sensing a certain amount of frustration similar to what had prompted us to start the Zac's Place journey. He too was asking questions, whether there was another way, whether the Church could learn to be multilingual and so be able to communicate much more widely across the community.

We stayed in touch, with me keeping him up to date with developments at Zac's Place. Meanwhile, he got the top job in the Anglican Church but still made the time to be interested in what we were doing when he was Archbishop of Canterbury, even though we didn't fall under the Anglican umbrella. One of the first missional agendas Rowan put on the table while at Canterbury was to see the establishment of a joint initiative with the Methodist Church called Fresh Expressions. Fresh Expressions has since grown to be an international movement involving many denominations and mission agencies; it is a serious attempt to plant new churches that are open to stripping back to basics and trying new things, and has met with a significant amount of success in many different contexts in several countries. It has also risen to the challenge of looking at additional ordination processes, away from the parish priest model and including more pioneering ministry roles.

Rowan acknowledges the significant inspiration that he and others have drawn from following projects and journeys such as ours in this regard, and never more so than in one of his farewell speeches as Archbishop of Canterbury in 2012. The seeds of change can so often begin on the margins and not at the centre. At times it was easy to think that we were fumbling around in the dark. Little did we know that those glimmers of light would attract the attention of some significant movers and shakers within the mainstream established Church. Rowan continues to be a tremendous encourager and takes the opportunity to call in when he's visiting his Swansea roots. I have also enjoyed numerous opportunities to engage with Fresh Expressions in various capacities in the years since.

Off the back of the TV programmes we rode a bit of a wave for a while. A local concert promoter provided us with the opportunity to host a second stage at a concert in the local Singleton Park. The iconic Motorhead were headlining the main stage. We presented some of our regular acts plus Chicago-based bluesman Glenn Kaiser and Sammy Horner's The Electrics. Duke Special in a previous incarnation also performed and The Alarm's Mike Peters headlined, much to the excitement of my wife, who performed with Lorraine immediately before

Mike took the stage. Such events were significant milestones – being invited into these environments and able to contribute something. It was not about getting our name known, but about a deepening of relationships in the city and earning the right to have a voice on things that would matter.

We continued to run our Sunday-night pub gatherings, although as they grew in popularity the dynamic began to change. We attracted crowds of around 150 people. It had become the cool place to hang out for Christian young people after they had been to a church gathering elsewhere. While many of these young people benefited, some established regulars felt lost in the crowd. Table banter started to be about things alien to them. It wasn't all bad, though. One young Christian lad who was pretty much on his way out of the back door of the church was encouraged to hang in there, and went on into ministry. He acknowledges that those times at Zac's Place kept him in the faith. But despite this, we needed to do something to halt the change in dynamic.

The pub we were using was struggling financially. Several managers had come and gone. When we turned up to use the function room we would discover the furniture as we had left it the previous week. It seemed like a good time to move on for several reasons. The influx of Christian tourists had caused us a problem and knocked things off centre a little. The best thing I could come up with for dealing with it was to move to one of the more raucous pubs in town. Just around the corner, The Office was under new management. They offered us the opportunity to shift our operations there. I assumed it would be in a function room, but it was actually in the main public bar, which added another dimension to the gatherings. Moving to a rock and roll, rough and ready bar resulted in all the Christian tourists who were there just for a post-church chat vanishing overnight, leaving us with our original core community of people. We also had the added dynamic of passing trade falling through the door who were out for a night on the town!

The Office years were a fascinating time. Using the public bar, we became part of the pub community. I conducted pastoral gatherings over lunch and would frequently find myself talking into the small hours with the bar staff long after the doors had closed. It wasn't uncommon for people to refer to the pub as the 'Jesus' pub. We wrote and produced simple monthly news sheets that were left on the bar not just on Sundays but all week. It started to become a bit of a biker hang-out after those of us at Zac's had been parking the Harleys outside. I took a wedding blessing there, and sadly also the funeral of a young regular who drank there. Often it seemed that an unofficial chaplaincy role in the pub was developing alongside our original intentions.

We had set out with the simple intentions of building relationships and nurturing people in their faith in Christ, so it seems reasonable to ask the question whether, despite the buzz of activity, it did actually achieve anything in those formative years. There's a danger when evaluating missional activity of being drawn into the numbers game. In all honesty, I have absolutely no idea how many people we have connected with over the years, nor how many we have assisted in their journey to find faith in Christ. I have no idea how many people we have encouraged to hang on in there, to just keep going despite everything they are fighting through. Nor do I have any idea how many people we may have put off along the way, and while I am sure there are a few, I hope and trust not too many. But what I do know is this: we received enough encouragement, reaction and signs of fruit in barren places to keep going. Although we received criticism from some Christian brothers and sisters, in the fullness of time many have come to see that we brought something of value to some people.

The stories are in the lives of ordinary people we met in the bar in those formative years. Throughout the entire history of Zac's Place thus far, people have been involved for varying lengths of time. Some are wanderers passing through, some are with us for a season and some stick closer than a lonely dog and never disappear. Marcus came to us in the very early days, bruised and battered from some tough experiences. His fear of crowds meant that he would stay in the lobby for ages before finding the confidence to walk in. Fifteen years on, Marcus is an essential wise voice in our Zac's Place community. His health issues have meant that it's always been difficult for him to work, but in his staunch support and commitment to the weakest members of our community he has found value and meaning because he's accepted and loved.

Martin was similar in that his faith in Christ was real though he had been burned by the Church. Travelling from the Rhondda Valley each week, he put in serious miles to take in what was happening in those early years, and to feed his soul on the community there, especially receiving support when his daughter went through the trauma of drug addiction. Many years on, he's part of God's Squad, he's one of the most consistent voices at Zac's Place and has been a dedicated community chaplain in the local prison, working with some of the most alienated and prolific repeat offenders. At Zac's Place, all we have ever tried to do is give a warm welcome and offer people, whoever they are, an opportunity to be themselves, together with the space and confidence to bring what they carry in their heart and be open to the tenderness and grace of God at work in people as fragile as they are.

It often makes for a bizarre mix of flavours, a simmering casserole of oddities, but that's what makes it taste so good. A decent wine is formed under immense pressure, squeezing every last drop of flavour out. Far too often church, and some other relational experiences for that matter, can seem like the momentary collision of pool balls that then retreat in opposite directions to their separate pockets.

I cannot ignore the beautiful connections we have made with a wide network of very creative people. A huge number of musicians found a new lease of energy and life exercising their creativity in the communal spaces we formed. People who hadn't written in years started writing songs again, an entire musical was written, recorded and performed, poets had the chance to add their voice to the mix and musicians who previously had only been playing in religious events took their music to bars and radio stations. There was a tremendous buzz of creativity and deep mutual respect and encouragement to try new things. The art of storytelling was embraced; for many just to be able to hang out together without anyone looking on making ill-conceived judgemental comments was a breath of fresh air.

Artists in my experience are some of the most misunderstood people both within the Church and in wider society. The artistic spirit is often chaotic and unpredictable. They sense, see and feel things in a very different way from everyone else. Sometimes the artist will pick up on the vibe of a shifting culture long before anyone else does. They'll be the ones bellowing out the warning shots, asking the awkward questions, giving voice to an anger that's bubbling under the surface or screaming with the pain of a tormented and troubled generation. They are also possibly more likely than anyone else to struggle to keep relationships together, live on an even keel – and to drop the 'f' bomb in a church meeting! They'll perhaps be on an emotional roller coaster of euphoria one minute and extreme depression the next, but never underestimate the contributions of the poet, the actor, the songwriter, the sculptor or the dancer.

Because of these varied experiences of creative people and the Church sometimes being reluctant to be open to their voice, their gift has often been wasted and vastly underused. The value of the extrovert orator preaching week in week out is, let's face it, considered far more valuable than the deeply introverted artist, who presents us not so much with answers as with questions about the way the world is and how messy things are. The voice of the artist is a valid and necessary one in society, yet within the Church it is a travesty that so many creative voices are muzzled, restricted to twee presentations, beige contemporary worship and creative token gestures.

I am not suggesting that people don't do these things with the utmost conviction, but I do suggest that we are severely restricting the number of prominent flavours we permit in the casserole of church. We are not only selling ourselves short, we are potentially missing the still small voice of God in the rasps, tones, groans, textures, sounds, images and moves of artists, made in the image of their creator. If you want to spice up the casserole of church, then embrace the poor and give voice to artists and creative thinkers, unleash their creativity and passion. It will never be the same again.

The idea of gathering in a bar certainly created a good platform for fostering relationships. Against the backdrop of some seriously fine music from songwriters that genuinely connected with what we were doing, a constant drip-feeding of relevant, punchy, topical, biblical anecdotes brought some backbone and threw topics and issues out there for dialogue. Gradually we formed a cohesive, diverse community of people in varying states of chaos and occasional stability who not only cared for each other but were becoming serious about what it meant to be a follower of Jesus, and were asking to share in the sacraments of communion and baptism.

Eventually, though, the inevitable happened and the 'Church in a Pub' ran its course. While the pub was a great place to meet people, it wasn't the best venue for everybody and certainly not suited to disciple those for whom an environment that offered alcohol was less than beneficial. Something needed to change as the challenges of discipleship appeared to be in conflict with frontier mission.

11

Crossing borders

———— ·•·•· ————

On a Sunday afternoon I would often find myself riding back along the M4 motorway, having been on the road with God's Squad at a motorcycle event somewhere in Britain, or maybe in Ireland or elsewhere, getting back for our Zac's Place gathering in the pub. I'd usually be exhausted with my face covered in road dirt, the smoke of a clubhouse 200 miles away still lingering in my hair.

The first ten years of establishing God's Squad in Europe was a time of steady growth. We had about a dozen members spread around England, Wales and Ireland and more invitations than we could handle to visit a multitude of motorcycle clubs on a regular basis. These visits would be to custom motorcycle events, bars and, more significantly, clubhouses, where the only way to gain access is by personal invitation. Do anything disrespectful, though, and you are shown the door in no uncertain terms. Maintaining close connections with the chapters of the club in Australia and New Zealand was also important. The emergence of email and the internet certainly made this a lot easier, cheaper and more accessible for everyone. Smithy was still making regular visits to the UK in between completing his doctorate in Kentucky at Asbury Seminary, and I made it a priority to develop the personal links at the Aussie end, with biannual visits. One of these included my accepting the offer of ordination in 2002 at God's Squad's home church at the time, St Martin's in Melbourne, an independent denomination of earthy community churches.

The internet also meant that other people in other countries could find us more easily. If the growth of God's Squad in the 1980s was primarily down to John Smith's books and his regular speaking tours and missions, then the internet was a big factor in our formative growth into Europe. This presented an early challenge for us and to a certain extent that challenge still exists.

The attraction for me about God's Squad was missional. There was a deeply theological challenge and methodology of mission that made sense. It wasn't just a strapline with a couple of images of unkempt blokes on their Harleys on a web page. It was about getting involved in the nitty-gritty of a subculture, engaging with it in a manner I believed Christ would. Smithy carried the spirit of John Wesley's Methodism, emphasizing the importance of being on the road, the proclamation of the gospel, advocating for the rights of the poor and discipling people in small groups. This is certainly part of the DNA of God's Squad, and as the ministry of God's Squad has grown internationally, the task of retaining the core DNA continues to be a priority.

There has always been a radical gospel edge to the club, but the risk that it could degenerate into a holding pen for those within the Church looking for a place to rebel is a serious one. Indeed, many Christian motorcycle clubs, including God's Squad, can be a credible way to function in an admirable ministry, but risk being used as a route for men to ignore dealing with other responsibilities at home or within their lives. Seemingly credible ministry can be a seductive mistress sometimes. Part of my ongoing role has been to repeatedly remind people of our core mission and sometimes call into question a member's motives.

Soon we were making connections with what we hoped would be similar-minded people in Norway, Finland, Ireland, Germany, Ukraine, Holland and the Baltic countries. We began the very long process of actually getting to know these men and their families. God's Squad colours have never been handed out cheaply and they never will. I knew more than anyone of the cost and testing of the call to the club across many miles, so there was no way we were going to dilute our missional ethos for the sake of quick and impressive expansion into Europe.

Early on in our European interactions we received an email from a young student in Kiev, Ukraine. He was studying at theology school for youth ministry but felt a strong calling to minister among bikers. He and his brother were into their bikes and the newfound freedom that Ukraine was enjoying meant that motorcycle clubs were now becoming established. It was like the 1950s, 1960s and 1970s happening all at once as Western ideas flooded in. One of his lecturers was an Australian who was familiar with God's Squad back home and he suggested the student contact us. Our Sydney chapter received an email in broken English from Pasha and over the next few years he doggedly persisted in communication, determined to begin God's Squad with his brother. Tragically, his brother drowned in a swimming accident, but Pasha was undeterred and we enabled him to come and join in our UK tenth-anniversary celebrations in 2005. He made a three-day bus ride to get there, as his $20 Ukrainian bike probably would not have completed the journey. We finally met a young man whose zeal to serve Christ was impressive and who would later prove to be essential in the foundation of the first Ukrainian chapter of God's Squad. The move into Eastern Europe, which has since included Lithuania, Estonia and Poland, presented fresh challenges, but also additional opportunities to enrich further the flavour of this unlikely lay mission movement.

We have endeavoured to hold true to the core values of God's Squad, which are, simply, to attempt to connect with our biker mates and others on the margins. The others on the margins have always been a significant part. My experience of beginning Zac's Place and the growing diverse mix of marginalized friends was replicating in only a slightly different way how the Melbourne chapter had initially grown in the early 1970s at the height of the Jesus Movement.

A growing number of God's Squad chapters around the world have planted mission churches on the margins. The biker subculture is a priority area of focus for the club, but we don't stop there. God's Squad members often work alongside prisoners, addicts, young people and the homeless, championing the causes of those whose voices get lost in the noise. We might be one of the most diverse lay ministries on the planet, as an international gathering of God's Squad members demonstrates. With a mix of Jesus Movement hippy survivors, Methodists, Anglicans, Catholics, Baptists, Lutherans, Eastern Orthodox, Salvation Army, Pentecostals, Coptics and Evangelicals to name a few, there can be no doubt that the flavour is full-bodied and full of surprises!

While on the surface there may be a hundred and one reasons to divide us, the shared vision and active ministry on the road, and on the margins, is the cohesion that bonds us together. It's a journey of ongoing discipleship with a commitment to Christ and his call that will not be diluted. Our members include clergymen, high-flying businessmen and academics. We have surgeons, aircraft engineers, and also those who struggle to hold down a job on minimum wage. Some love a whisky and a cigar, others are teetotal, some are covered in tattoos and piercings, others can't see the point of getting ink. The Eastern Europeans and Scandinavians will be comfortable to sit naked in a clubhouse sauna together, while the Aussies are petrified at the thought! Diversity in culture and life experience is a wonderful thing when the foundations are clearly defined and are able to support such a glorious mix. Each person comes into the club with different things to learn; that's why the process is a long one. Each member knows that by the time they are granted their colours, their calling has been tested, their motives quizzed and their commitment verified.

The challenge is to continue to earn the right to speak into the lives of the people we spend our time with. It remains essential not to dilute the radical missional edge that embraces the marginalized; we need to keep retelling the stories that pull everything into sharp focus and to stay out on the road and on the margins, which is where so much of Jesus' ministry recorded in the Gospels takes place.

This challenge comes sharply to the fore when we set up a new chapter in a new country. Setting out our stall right from the beginning is vital, but it is not always easy where matters of language, culture, local bike-scene politics and attitudes towards the Church all come into play. For example, the opinion people will have towards the Church from an Irish perspective – there are victims of abuse by priests within clubs there – will colour how you are perceived even before you have opportunity to speak. Occasionally you find yourself having to go in to bat on a very rough wicket.

Sometimes the opportunities to engage in conversation come easily. In the formative days of us setting up in Eastern Europe there was a welcome from several of the clubs to their clubhouses. I travelled on my own to meet with our contact there, who fortunately had a good grasp of English. Behind locked doors and in fortified darkened clubhouses, he translated my words as I made our case for wanting to begin a chapter of God's Squad in their country. Of course, we could just start without this diplomacy, but there is little point riding roughshod over subcultural codes if you expect to come out of the experience with defining friendships and influence. On such occasions I am hoping my simple phrases are being translated well as I sit with senior officers and partake of their hospitality. It may be a coffee, or a meal, it may be we are all sitting naked in a sauna enjoying a beer. In one scenario, it was in a secure windowless meeting room, with a tray of shot glasses every 15 minutes filled with some seriously strong home-brewed chilli vodka. These shots were interspersed with the local delicacy of cubes of fat mixed with pickled gherkins. I've never been so glad to see gherkins in all my life! These forays into foreign territory become important staging posts in building open friendships, which in turn pave the way for us to develop as a ministry. Accepting hospitality when it is given, whether it suits your taste or not, is all part of building bridges.

Bridge-building should never be about arriving in a blaze of glory. It is about quietly showing respect, appreciating hospitality, honouring the relationships that our local contacts have already developed on the ground, and earning the right to speak. One of my last responsibilities as an international officer of the club was to attend the party for one of our European chapters when they were granted God's Squad membership status. What an encouragement it was to see every club in that nation send representation to the party at the God's Squad clubhouse and what a privilege to thank them for giving us the space to do what we do. How fitting it was, too, to receive a gift of a Bible from one of the clubs, for our own clubhouse, and a classy bottle of red wine accompanied by a note explaining that we'd find the instructions on what to do with the 'sacramental' wine in the Bible! This tongue-in-cheek humour typifies the underlying genuine respect that can be established with those who do not necessarily share our faith but are open to seeing where we fit within their subculture.

It isn't always as straightforward as this, though. In another scenario, it took nearly ten years of engaging with local clubs as the complexities of club politics played out. Repeated lengthy road trips, often at short notice, not only put miles on my bike, it gave opportunities to build strong personal connections – but it also tested the patience of the emergent chapter.

Sometimes it could be a hostile environment we would be entering, depending on what else was being discussed that evening. I would walk into the meeting room when the allotted time came and one by one different clubs would voice their support, opposition or genuine enquiry as to why we would want to establish a chapter of God's Squad on their doorstep. Questions usually come with an intensity that allows no room for a weak-willed response. The clubs are seeking something of substance, what defines who we are, not who we could be pretending to be. Many of these men are former soldiers and they can tell if the wool is being pulled over their eyes and you are something other than who you claim to be.

Eventually there comes a breakthrough, and in these moments our difference as being followers of Christ becomes both a challenge and a cause of fascination. As new sets of colours go up, we truly nail our colours to the mast and there is no place to hide. We've won the respect of the local subculture to do so, whether it takes three years or ten, but it is then up to our members on the ground to live in the light of that responsibility, develop the mission locally and continue to earn the right to speak and serve in ministry with humility and grit.

On days when I have felt like giving up, when the politics grinds me down, when an abusive bully tries to humiliate me or when I think, quite frankly, I'm not sure whether I can still do this after so many years, I ask myself what it is that keeps me going. Within the context of God's Squad, it's the stories: stories about people, about the deep sense of loyalty and mutual respect found in sometimes surprising places, but in a manner that you know can only have been a God-ordained encounter.

In the early days of making connections with clubs there were many who really didn't want to know me or my travelling companions. The 'persona non grata' attitude did not come from just one corner. There was a fair bit of ribbing and joking at our expense, but interestingly often the jokes were a bit of a back-handed compliment.

There was one guy I kept bumping into around the different bike events and shows. He was in a club and also a trader selling biking apparel. Over the years we struck up a good friendship. He understood where I was coming from, and what God's Squad was aiming to achieve. He became an important advocate within his circle for our cause and privately encouraged and supported us, while publicly giving me a hard time. His marriage and his business both faltered, a couple of his club brothers and good friends died, and he had several bike accidents; and each time he was drawn to talk these things through with me away from the noise of the clubhouse, sometimes at his home and occasionally on the hospital ward.

I have learned that even in mission, friendships work both ways. At one time I would not have considered that any so-called 'non-believing' friend of mine could ever do anything to support or encourage me, but how wrong I was. In times of conflict he would be a diplomatic voice behind the scenes to smooth things over, and he was actually a significant man of peace on our behalf on several occasions. Trust and respect worked both ways despite our apparent differences in lifestyles and our very different patches.

Many years into our friendship, he was diagnosed with terminal cancer. This came as devastating news, naturally, although not a complete surprise. He had lost his mother at a similar age to cancer. His life was sometimes chaotic, though what stability he did have he had no hesitation in attributing to his club membership. Apparently, his father used to admit that it was only being in the club that kept his son alive and out of prison. That's why it grieves me so much when politicians take cheap shots at bike clubs. For many, it's a simple fact of finding somewhere to belong. A smart misfit is far less of a liability in a structured tribe than he would be running loose.

As my friend's health deteriorated, he reached an impressive anniversary milestone for membership of his club. These occasions are celebrated and marked with parties that can go on for days, and gifts may be forthcoming from brothers in different chapters. In God's Squad around the world we have been blessed with a number of exceptionally talented artists. It's not uncommon for us to organize the gift of a portrait painted by one of our members either of an individual member of a club for such an occasion or of a whole club for an anniversary, maybe in memory of a departed member. Magoo is one of those artists. His unbelievably lifelike portraits hang in a multitude of clubhouses around the world. His ability to capture someone's personality is quite exceptional and has brought many a grizzled biker to tears. His talent is only matched by his humility and generosity of heart.

This gift was no exception. Magoo graciously came up with a stunning portrait and as we presented it to my friend of 20 years, he stood in silence at the bar. His face was now beginning to show the rigours of cancer treatment and symptoms. He ran his fingers over the textured paint noting the detail – Magoo had even included the small scars from chemotherapy treatment. He was overwhelmed and acknowledged that in his whole life, this had possibly been the most moving of surprises.

He returned to his small flat, where he promptly hung the portrait of himself on the wall, directly above the fireplace, opposite his couch. As his symptoms worsened he became more housebound and not a day went by without him being moved by the gift of this painting. We kept in touch regularly. It wasn't easy for me to make the long journey to see him, so he would send messages updating me, knowing full well that I would be in prayer for him. I promised I would make the journey to see him again, and I did.

It was an emotionally charged evening for lots of reasons, which aren't for the pages of this book – they are too personal – but I had previously decided I wasn't going to leave for home without offering to share a prayer with my friend. This was going to be the last time I expected to see him before he lost consciousness. It wasn't as straightforward as you might think, as there were other club brothers there too, but when I offered to pray with him he accepted, and his brothers respectfully gave us some privacy.

We sat at his small kitchen table, with the background noise of his oxygen supply gently hissing every few breaths. I thanked

God for the friendship we had shared and asked that the Lord himself would meet us at our point of deepest need. I shared honest words on how I felt and how I thought he was probably feeling as he knew his days were running out. In the moments that followed, I truly believe that he found peace with God, as he mustered a wholehearted 'Amen' with what little breath he had.

All the questions over the years, all the mocking, the mutual respect, everything the journey of life had brought us for good and ill came to rest in moments of solitude and tears of gratitude. I made one more trip to see him a few days later, at the request of his brothers, and sat by his bed in some of his final hours. At his request, and with complete freedom to share my heart, a few weeks later I laid his mortal body to rest in the company of hundreds of his club brothers, family and friends, with a precious confidence that all was well with his soul.

If I had given up at the first sign of a beating, I would not have friendships of 20 years and longer to celebrate. If collectively we had given up at the first sign of persecution, we would never have been in a position to weave threads of redemptive justice, mercy and humility into a complex tapestry of tribalism, where aspects of the ancient virtues reminiscent of Greek and Trojan heroes still exist, particularly physical strength, courage, cunning, brotherhood and honour. If I had not had the company of some of the best travelling companions on the planet, we would not have lasted the journey and experienced the growth we have. This has never been about lone characters blazing a trail out front; we function best as a community of walking wounded on a shared adventure.

In 2007 I wrote the following words to accompany my threadbare original God's Squad colours, which were cased up and returned home to God's Squad Melbourne chapter as a gift for their thirty-fifth anniversary.[4]

These colours

These colours are a milestone.
They tell a story that unfolds across the globe.
These colours are an object of desire.
They've been welcomed by some, they've been a target too.
Through the media lens, the envious eye of a friend,
The embrace of a brother and the eyes of one who would
 bring us ill.
As followers of Christ, the gift of grace is just that, a gift;
But these colours were earned.
These colours are a statement of sacrifice;
Of brotherhood, of mission, of commitment to the Call.
They've been marinated in life on the road,
In clubhouses, jails and bars.
Ingrained with road dirt, fuel and smoke from a thousand
places,
Nations far and wide;
The tears of the broken-hearted, the imprint of the
aggressors' hands,
As we've sought to take a stand for what we believe is right
and just.
They carry the blood of my veins, that of others,
And they continue to represent the spilt blood of One far
greater,
Who by his grace continues to enable the crimson tide of
change in ordinary lives.
These colours have returned home;
To the place of vision and of trust
And in celebration that we continue to be united
And are able to do much more together
Than we ever could on our own.

12

Scrambled eggs

Some days it was a festival stage, some days a clubhouse. Occasionally a radio interview and sometimes a pulpit. Maybe a prison or perhaps the Baptist Ladies' Guild meeting! Sometimes on the bike, sometimes on an Airbus. A Ukrainian police station or a slum community. Life became an interesting diverse mix of opportunity and learning to communicate on many levels. But wherever I was and whatever else was happening, the gatherings at Zac's Place were fixed points in the diary. While we'd had a good run in the pubs, it was becoming apparent we needed to look for some additional options to gather people together who were wanting more. We had some folk with serious alcohol issues and the pub wasn't the best place for them.

Mary came to us deeply troubled. We met her in the bar initially and she kept coming to our gatherings over a number of years. Her story was one of immense heartache and pain, and initially she didn't want to talk much about it. She had talked so many times before, to so many people, the thought of opening up the wounds again was almost too difficult to bear. She had been passed around a few different counsellors when she had sought help, but many issues remained unresolved, leaving her with the impression that her problems were too big to handle. She was volatile on occasions, had a problem with alcohol and regularly fell out with her neighbours. She trusted very few people but was drawn to the warmth of our gatherings. Gradually over time she began to tell her story in tiny pieces, often in riddles and at times when I least expected it. In all honesty some of the time I didn't know what to believe and what not to believe, so confusing were the fragments of information. Eventually she told me why she would never go back to a church.

She explained how the leaders in her church had thought she was possessed by a demon. Without any explanation, or invitation from her, they gathered around her to pray, stretched out their hands to place on her and started shouting at this apparent demonic influence. It petrified the poor woman, and not only that, it raised an ugly part of her story to the surface.

One of the reasons she was so traumatized was because long before this she had been the victim of a satanic ritual that had abused her in a most horrific way. While I am sure those church leaders were well meaning in their approach, their methods did nothing to help bring any kind of healing and cleansing. Imagine for a brief moment how you would feel if, carrying all the pain that had been inflicted on you by men you should have been able to trust, you were then thrust into a closed circle of male church leaders, all placing their hands on you and shouting. I really do not care whether they terminated their prayers with a fervent 'in the name of Jesus'; there is no way this was ever going to be the tender work of the sweet spirit of Jesus bringing healing and restoration to a most fragile soul.

I sometimes tell stories such as Mary's on the road when speaking at church communities. Quite rightly it provokes revulsion and shock, but so often this sort of thing is done in church without much thought. Sometimes glib remarks are made, or jokes at others' expense that may seem innocent are placed in a sermon, but these can have far-reaching, damaging effects that sometimes we never know about, because quite simply people walk out and never come back.

Over the years I have disciplined myself to assume that in every gathering I speak at, in whatever context, there will be someone there who has been raped. There is someone there who was orphaned, someone in the raw stages of recent grief, someone contemplating suicide, someone who's a secret addict, someone who can't forgive themselves for the pain they have caused others, someone convinced they have committed the unforgivable sin. So the list goes on. If as a Church we say we are there for the weakest and most vulnerable, then we need to assume that that is everyone's starting point, regardless of what we are presented with when they walk through the door.

Over time, I met with Mary with the support of a trusted female counsellor connected with our ministry. We agreed to meet for several sessions and talked through her trauma with a view to seeing her released from all the ties that bound her. We decided how long each session would last and we agreed in advance what areas of discussion we would cover so there would be no surprises. We promised her that neither of us would raise our voice and neither of us would touch her or stand over her.

What followed was a very precious time of healing and liberation. In the end, there were demonic influences present that needed to be dealt with. It was one of very few instances when I have felt I have been talking directly to the demonic. It was not Mary's voice that responded on several occasions, but when we instructed the demonic influence to leave her body, we commanded it to leave silently, without causing convulsions or throwing Mary around the room, as I had previously seen.

We were praying to the sovereign God, to whom even the demons have to submit, so we wanted to make sure that this demonic influence didn't just leave, it left in the manner we told it to. In Mary's recollection of those moments it was like a butterfly leaving her body: a moment of release that allowed peace to reign, way beyond our limits of understanding. Shortly after this she chose to be baptized, which we did, and she continues to follow Jesus in the light of the burden lifted. For her, Zac's Place was an important staging post; we met her in complete turmoil at a time when all other options had come to a dead end. She now has found her place in another church community where there aren't quite so many chaotic people, and no one deserves a quieter life more than her.

There were others like Mary who needed a safe place to grow in their faith. We considered buying an old pub at one stage, with the idea of running a licensed music venue upstairs to fund a city centre mission initiative at street level downstairs. We drew up a business plan, but the money required was way beyond anything we could lay our hands on and the venue we were looking at was taken off the market as plans for redeveloping Swansea city centre made it more viable for the brewery to hang on to it. It just never really came together but as we continued our Sunday night pub gatherings I knew in my gut that we needed to enter a new phase.

At the same time, I needed to find some storage and office space as the arrangement I had had with the Baptist church came to an end. A temporary option became available at an old Gospel Hall in the city centre. It was one of many churches, halls and chapels that have closed in recent years, and had been out of use for about two years. A small elderly congregation just weren't able to sustain the upkeep and it must have been a tough call when the doors were locked for the last time. Previously a vibrant church community had been based there, with thriving children's Sunday schools and youth work.

As soon as I walked into the space, I knew that this was the building we had been looking for. The big hall with a balcony would lend itself to music events, and there was a smaller meeting room that I could already envisage being made into something that resembled a bar, but without the booze. Other rooms could be used as office and storage space and it was right in the centre of the city. The only drama was that as a charity we only had about £2,000 in the bank, mostly owed to the tax office.

In spite of this we came to an arrangement to purchase the building, at a reduced price but still significantly more than we had, and therefore without knowing where we would find the money. We have had over many years a loyal support base of friends and church connections. One supporter was prepared to be a guarantor on the mortgage we would need, and we managed to raise enough extra to cover the payments. It was the sort of story that usually happened to other people! Somehow, out of nothing and less than six months after first walking through the doors of the Gospel Hall, we had bought it. Zac's Place – Church in a Pub? began the journey of transformation to Zac's Place – A Church for Ragamuffins! The building itself, though, has never defined what or who the church is; it is a shell that serves as a base for a community of people who are the church.

Despite the almost miraculous manner in which we were able to acquire the building, shortly after moving in there was a sting in the tail. At the very time our outgoings had increased to pay the mortgage on the property, which was still less than if we had been renting a small office and store, we lost the financial help of both our supporting Baptist churches, which amounted to more than our additional outgoings.

It was bizarre that both churches ceased at the same time and I don't think for one minute there was any collusion. It's just the way it worked out. Personnel and priorities change and very few people in either of those church communities had been there when Jayne and I were initially supported in ministry many years before. But it still prompted a certain amount of grieving, as these were the places that had nurtured us in the faith.

A small team of Zac's regulars got stuck in with renovating the parts of the building we wanted to bring into use. The drama school that Jayne had been running moved their classes into the main hall almost immediately. Some theatre groups rehearsed there and we invited local community groups to use the space. For our own specific missional purposes, we continued to run the pub nights in tandem with beginning a new weekly Zac's Place communal meeting and Bible study we called a Tribal Gathering at our newly acquired headquarters. Initially we met on a weekday lunchtime as most people were out of work, but we soon moved it to a Tuesday evening, where it has continued to thrive and be a regular fixed point in our calendar. However, before this became well established, our significant new priority was to ascertain whether we could use the space to meet some of the needs for the city's most vulnerable.

A venue was needed for providing breakfast for the homeless, working in partnership with local agencies who cared for those who were sleeping rough in the city. Up until that point the churches would do their thing and the council-connected agencies would do theirs. There wasn't a huge amount of dialogue and this became an opportunity to bridge a gap. It proved to be a good move and has been of massive benefit to us all, especially our vulnerable friends. Many years on, we have not only a good working relationship with homeless agencies in the city, drugs projects and medical professionals but also deep respect and personal friendships with many of the staff. Cohesive partnerships across the city are vital and we have been able to maintain our identity as a church community – in particular, a church community that supports the homeless and vulnerable.

There was also a gap on a Thursday to provide a free hot meal, so very shortly after we had bought the hall we started opening up on a Thursday evening. Sometimes it was just two of us, essentially me and Bryan Roberts, running a soup kitchen. Bryan had been voluntarily operating a church soup kitchen and soup run in the city for the best part of 20 years until it was closed down. He knew the majority of the street community and everyone loved him, and that connection soon brought a regular crowd into our emerging space.

Nowadays we have a large team of volunteers to look after each coffee bar night, but early on it was manic: just a couple of us serving 30 people, a few dogs, sometimes a ferret and always nearly a punch-up. But quickly Zac's Place became established as somewhere people were welcomed and loved as they were. People respected the space. They knew it was all volunteer-led and running on donations, so the premises got looked after in the main. Street drinkers, psychotic addicts, folks with serious mental health issues and the simply lonely began to gravitate to us, some clutching sleeping bags under their arms, some collapsing as they fell through the door. Bryan's homemade 25-veg soup was a hit and so the soup kitchen gathered momentum in a similar way to the early Sunday nights in the pub.

It was more than just handing out soup, bathing wounds and supplying dry clothes. This was a serious act of worship in itself. This was treating each one of our guests as though they were Christ himself. I have met and engaged with the most beautiful people in the most unlikely places, and our coffee bar regulars have provided many such opportunities.

We have been involved in distributing food on the streets as well, and one such occasion was a Thursday night in December, and it was biting cold. It was the day before Black Friday. Before the phrase was hijacked by North American consumerism, Black Friday was the name given to the last working Friday before Christmas and generally when a large number of the city's working population will be on the town for a party, drink and dance. Swansea has a thriving and le-gendary night life, and one of its biggest industries revolves around the consumption of alcohol; the council have issued large numbers of licences in a compact area of the city centre to encourage this. In recent years the relaxing of bar opening times means that most nights of the week a few streets are packed with revellers, though especially at weekends. Black Friday is one of the busiest nights of the year.

A local policy was often introduced at Christmas time to remove the apparent riff-raff from the most festive streets. These streets are popular haunts for those who sleep rough, beg or busk, as well as partygoers. But come Christmas, the clean-up happens to make way for a supposedly more respectable breed of working binge-drinker.

I was on the soup run and trying to catch up with a few friends who may have evaded the police patrols, when I found Bob. He sat amid a pile of boxes and black bags partially hidden behind a bin. He shuffled up and made some room for me and I poured us both some soup. The wind was perishing cold and I'm a great believer in sharing food with friends whenever possible, so I was glad to have a soup myself. We tucked down out of the wind and also the gaze of passing police patrols and had a good catch-up. Bob had his soup in one hand, a flagon of cider in the other and most of an earlier sandwich in his beard.

As I was talking to him I realized his attention had been caught elsewhere. We were sitting pretty much in the gutter and I struggled to see what he was looking at across the street. The cobbles of Wind Street were full of bare tottering legs, crowned with short skirts and precariously balanced on high heels. Interspersed were guys looking as if they were trying to carry a bus under each arm, gently swaggering from side to side with shirts unbuttoned. Through this staggering sea of bodies and shrieks of drunken laughter, I saw the object of Bob's attention. In an office doorway a young woman lay spreadeagled on the floor. She was wearing her little black party dress and had obviously spent some time fixing her hair and make-up before going out. But there she was, vomit running down her cleavage, her shoes long since discarded and now seemingly incapable of standing.

I stopped talking and looked back at Bob and one solitary tear ran from the corner of his eye, leaving a salty trail down his weather-beaten face into his matted beard. He gently shook his head muttering, 'It shouldn't have to be this way.' His heart was breaking for that young woman, whose dignity was in tatters and friends nowhere to be seen. The irony of this scenario, of course, lies in the fact that this was one of the men the local council wanted out of the way, because he made the place look untidy and he might be a pest. But in reality, he was seeing the world far more clearly than anyone else, from his vantage point in the gutter. Mother Teresa often used to say that 'the face of Jesus turns up in the most distressing disguises'. I would wholeheartedly endorse that sentiment.

As we finished our soup, the wave of tottering humanity thinned enough for us to glimpse that the steps were now empty. Somehow the girl had gone.

Bob died a couple of years after this. Not on the streets, but in a flat he had just moved into. I took his funeral and shared that same story; no one was surprised, because those of us who knew him were well aware that he had a heart of gold despite the heartache and chaos he lived in. He also had a wicked sense of humour and he would have been very proud to know how his funeral began.

As the hearse made its entrance to the crematorium, I called out of the warm waiting room the group of a dozen freezing cold and mostly alcohol-fuelled friends, whom I had brought to the funeral in a borrowed church minibus. They gathered in the entrance trying to look dignified in a slightly unsteady kind of way, until one of them reached forward to shake a friend's hand. Ordinarily this wouldn't have been a problem, except the friend had a cider in one hand while the other one was holding up his borrowed posh trousers. Needless to say, it was the trousers that were released. Bob arrived at his funeral with a proper half-mast salute from one of his best friends whose lily-white skinny-stick legs were topped and tailed by ill-fitting Y-fronts and borrowed trousers!

Colourful characters like Bob have often been conveyors of important truths to me. When we open our doors to the poor, we open our eyes to a new way of seeing and our hearts to a new way of learning. I don't think it's a coincidence that a significant amount of Jesus' recorded ministry in the Gospels was among the poor and the marginalized. When we took on the stewardship of our little building we wanted to send a very strong signal about who was important to us as a church community. It was always going to be the poor and the weak. We have gained a reputation for our support and work among the homeless, and have received some community recognition by way of awards, which we're very humbled by, but it confuses me. Our priorities are not odd or strange, they are ones we take straight out of the Gospels. The early Church took up offerings to feed the poor, not maintain an institution. Over the years I have been fortunate enough to gain a wide array of church experience. I have preached in just about every mainstream denomination you care to mention, in over a dozen countries, and many of these will be engaged in valuable work among the marginalized. But I do have to ask the question: for how many of us is our work among the poor a token gesture and for how many a serious priority and even an act of worship? One way of ascertaining this would be to look at how a church's budget is spent. Where its heart is, is generally where its money will be spent.

Eventually we decided to wind down the pub evenings. The Tuesday-night gatherings were taking off, while the dynamic at the pub was changing. My long-term sound-engineering genius, Paul, who had faithfully been part of the entire Zac's Place journey thus far, now had family commitments that he never thought would happen, and was no longer available. Many of the musicians were out gigging more, and I was simply exhausted. As much as I didn't want to stop running the pub gatherings, we had to. There would still be enormous value in returning to them – their impact in the city is still talked about and fondly remembered. Many of the folks with whom we are now involved we first met in the pub, but reality dawned that we needed to take care of those we had gathered along the way before looking to meet more people.

It's sometimes a long road from first meeting people to seeing them come to faith and discipling them. It can be a messy business, as some of the stories included here have indicated. If it took Jesus three years on the road with his ragamuffin bunch of misfits (and they were still pretty ragged round the edges) then why should we expect any shortcuts? The ongoing focus at Zac's Place is undoubtedly to be a friend of the outcast and to disciple those who want to be followers of Jesus. We don't have a fancy programme, we have an open door and an open Bible.

Our regular Tribal Gatherings retain a refreshingly simple format. It worries me that a lot of church communities hang their hat on a feelings-based faith. At Zac's Place I have constantly banged the drum for us to learn from the Scriptures, together. What did Jesus actually say and what did he do? Where did the humanity and the sacred collide in the lives of characters like David? Where did Paul find the courage to keep going and how did he learn to communicate across borders? Why did the more obvious religious folk seem to have such a hard time from Jesus? Does the heartache and pain of Lamentations have anything to say to us today? Let's flesh it out, let's discuss it, let's ask questions, let's argue. Let us learn together from each other by methodically going through passages in the Bible. Let us learn to dream of a better day to come – but in the meantime, what does it truly look like to hang on to those virtues of faith, hope and love?

It's been interesting to see the rise in new forms of church, and also interesting to observe that when people start trimming back the churchy element in order to become more attractional to those who would not normally get involved, it's often the Bible that gets squeezed out. Technology comes in, music and graphics are modernized, venues are chosen because they're cool, and slowly but surely the dynamism of wrestling with the old book and applying it have been put on the back burner in favour of fleeting trends.

We have tended to do the opposite, which I think has been key in keeping us on track theologically and relationally. We regularly and methodically work through specific books of the Bible together, or maybe on a theme based around a particular character, such as David. We will make sure that each year a Gospel is covered, or a significant theme in one of the Gospels. It may be the Sermon on the Mount, the 'I am' sayings of Jesus, or the parables, but more often than not we will cover an entire book. We spent the best part of one year going through the Acts of the Apostles.

As always, we gather around a collection of small tables and on stools at the counter. We open with a short prayer and explain for any newcomers what the format is. Volunteers take it in turns to read a few lines, which in itself can be very liberating. This is not restricted to those who can read well; anyone can volunteer to do this. There's something very beautiful about seeing someone, with the support of folk around them, knowing their literacy skills are minimal yet wanting to have a go.

Patiently the group will wait and encourage as necessary as the words may be stumbled over and sometimes given comical twists, but the reading becomes a communal journey of discovery. Whoever is chairing the gathering will throw out some questions and we'll have a rough idea of what track we want the study to take and what the key points will be at the end. Someone will always have an opinion or a question, everyone is given space to contribute if they want to, and mutual respect is expected. Everyone is learning at a different pace and the education can come from unexpected sources. It's not uncommon for someone to be sitting face down at the table, seemingly out of it, maybe having had a wrap of heroin just before coming in or exhausted from being out in the cold. Just when you think the person is not listening, they will raise their head and bring an insight or a question that has everyone enthused.

The wonderful thing about opening up the Scriptures with each other in this way is that it gives the community room to breathe. It gives space for people to tell their stories, especially when they know that no one will laugh or be shocked at the tale they tell. It beggars belief that even within the Church the biblical narrative is not fully explored together as a community.

It is a mesmerizing mix of human experiences colliding with the eternal, revealing the threads of redemption in the most unlikely of places, people and circumstances. Human behaviour has changed little over the generations. At the core of our being we are fragile creatures, wanting to be loved, accepted and know peace. But we are dogged by an ability to be greedy, selfish, warmongering, paranoid and wallowing in bitterness and self-pity. We are our own worst enemy. That is the story of Adam, Noah, Abraham, Moses, Gideon, Daniel, David, Samson, Joseph and so many other characters whose lives unfold and unravel in the Bible. Peter, Thomas, Judas, John and Paul, all are up there with big fat loser potential. But they are in the story because they are just like the rest of us.

As we explore these stories and these characters, trying to understand the cultural context, we see something of ourselves. I'm not sure what Bible people are reading when they say it's not relevant. It becomes a travesty of truth, if as church communities we cannot effectively engage with the biblical narrative in a way that the weakest brother or sister can understand. We discover time and time again that it's not about always being right, it's about love, it's about faith in broken places, it's about mercy; it's about a bigger picture of a creator that is still in love with his creations and wants to see us reflect more of his glory. The narrative of the Bible remains one of the best tools to understand this never-ending love story.

The gatherings have a formal ending with a blessing. Sometimes, depending on the dynamic, there will be some communal prayer and maybe we will share the elements of communion, which will include non-alcoholic wine and not generally from a shared cup, as many of our number are in recovery and conditions like hepatitis are not uncommon. Over the years, we have always shared food together. It may be a meal, or perhaps homemade cakes. As time has gone on I increasingly agree with the sentiments of Salvation Army brothers and sisters who treat each meal as a sacred act of breaking bread together. But however we do it, Christ is remembered and the impact of his sacrificial death and the evidence of his resurrection in our fragile lives cannot and must not be ignored.

The informal conversations, whether they happen around the tables, outside or at the counter before and after, continue to be as important as when we first started to meet in the pub, because it's about a community of people, talking, sharing, laughing and crying together.

It may not look like an obvious church community from a brief glance. Some will be having a smoke out the front, motorcycles are parked outside, mugs of coffee sit on the window sill. Inside there'll be a mixed bag of people huddled around small old bar tables, while others stand or sit at a wooden counter. There's some God's Squad paraphernalia around and in the adjoining room, if you get that far, there are some striking pieces of artwork, notably Doris, the affectionate name given to a life-size sculpture that sits in the corner. If you look at the aforementioned tables you'll see some Bibles and the air will smell of all sorts. It may be homemade cake or it might be wet dog. There might be someone asleep at one of the tables; another person might be trying on some trainers. The lads outside the front might be stroking their beards pontificating on the finer points of an engineering dilemma and those inside will be comparing anti-psychotic medication and heart attacks. Someone will have a new tattoo or new teeth, someone will know someone who's just died and it will be someone's birthday and Liz will have made a cake. In short, it will look like a normal bunch of people from all walks of life, but it might not look like church.

The open nature of our gatherings, as the story of Jenny that opened the book demonstrates, means that they can be hijacked. We have some rules and boundaries, and if necessary we ask people to pipe down or leave if they become abusive or threatening, especially to more vulnerable members of the group.

Baz made it his ministry to take such people aside to calm them down. Baz was a doorman and a reliable, staunch member of God's Squad for a number of years before his sudden death in 2012 (which left us all heartbroken). All I would have to do was give him the nod of agreement and he would gently, but with persuasion, take our disruptive guest by the arm and lead them outside on the promise of a quiet chat and a cigarette. The offender would usually be someone we knew very well, and on other more sober occasions would be a very amenable part of the discussion. More often than not the person would be back inside for a coffee after the meeting had finished, and deeply apologetic. We always try to keep people included in the group and part of the community. If someone gets banned from the premises, we are usually the last in a long list of places in the city centre they have been banned from, and we will only do it if we think there is serious threat to the safety of others in our care. But even then, we do what we can to maintain the relationship and demonstrate our concern.

Our long-running Tribal Gatherings based around the Bible and food have been a constant source of inspiration and encouragement. It is the diversity of people that make up the community who make it what it is. I am so glad we didn't have a narrow focus on just being a biker church. It would have potentially become very bland and monotone. Of course, there are always bikes out the front and bikers coming and going.

In fact, a number of the local clubs actively support our efforts among the city's homeless by bringing clothes and food donations. Baz's funeral was a unique gathering which brought the worlds of Zac's Place and God's Squad together in a very poignant and tangible way.

There were about 400 bikes parked around the surrounding streets. We took the step of warning all our neighbours, a collection of very diverse ethnic and student communities, so as not to spring any surprises. There were clubs from many different places; assorted club patches were prominent amid the full turnout of God's Squad members from throughout the UK and others from overseas. Glenn came over from Australia to lead the tributes. And among the sea of bikers were the fragile souls from within our Zac's Place community, all with their own memories and stories to tell.

One of the traits about Zac's Place as a community is that our relationships have extended far beyond the formal gatherings and timetabled events. The ripples of connectedness and relationship extend across the city. There are those who get in touch when in crisis, others who love the artwork we have and like to bring friends to see it, and some who have been touched by the support they once received and like to keep in contact.

Lloyd is one who has always been around the periphery of Zac's Place ever since we began in the bar. He's a close personal friend these days and we've journeyed together through some desperate circumstances as well as some joyous ones, including the occasion of his wedding, which I conducted. Lloyd is an edgy artist who refuses to be pigeonholed on just about anything other than his love for Triumph motorcycles and his preferred medium of creativity, stained glass. Above one of the main doors of our venue is an example of his work and it serves as a distinctive creative example of an attempt to explain what goes on in this ramshackle old building.

The piece centres around our Zac's Place logo, a combination of complex Celtic knotwork and script, which was initially drawn freehand by Spike during a boring sermon. Lloyd sandblasted this design on to glass and then surrounded it with what looks like oddments of mismatched colours and shapes radiating out to the four corners. He had in fact searched under his work bench for his box of scraps, trial runs and off-cuts and made something beautiful out of previously rejected pieces. Carefully pieced together and illuminated, it is a striking piece of work capturing the complicated beauty and glorious chaos of Zac's Place. Beauty in brokenness remains a recurring theme.

Another way of describing the kind of Christian community that Zac's Place has developed into would be scrambled-egg church. I grew up in a church environment where the edges were clearly defined. It was everyone's business to know who was in and who was out, who believed what and who didn't. The yellow bits were yellow and the white bits were white and the church experience could be boiled or fried as long as the yoke wasn't punctured to blur the edges.

Boundaries are important, but not when they are enforced by judgemental attitudes instead of tender love and care. Take a brief look at Zac's Place and it's very difficult to work out who's who and where everyone's head may be at. We can be quick to make ill-conceived judgements and jump to conclusions on the basis of physical appearance, accent or body language in any group of people. You make that mistake at Zac's Place at your peril.

Liz has been a wonderful addition to our scrambled world. She performed poetry back in the early pub days, has always followed our progress and wrote a supportive piece for a Christian publication when we bought the hall. She didn't have a confident nature but eventually she plucked up courage to come and offer help, though she really wasn't sure if she would fit in. Nor was she certain how to help initially, but began to make cakes and helped serve teas and coffees while getting to know people. Liz was very self-conscious about being from the posh end of town and having a more refined accent, but that didn't matter as she was soon accepted and became an integral part of the family.

Liz wasn't expecting this. She had come to help poor, struggling people yet here she was striking up friendships with folk she thought she would be worlds apart from but in actual fact were just the same as her. Sure, they might have lived in a squat and have a history of drug abuse and prostitution, but there was something deeper that made it level ground. Liz soon realized that the people she had come to help were the ones who were feeding her soul and challenging her faith. She gradually found confidence and security, where often she had felt ignored or judged elsewhere. Now she brought her creativity to the group, helping us to write psalms and regularly leading the discussion; most of all for Liz, she had found somewhere to belong that accepted her as she was and gave her opportunity to flourish in ways she had not thought possible.

When Jesus encouraged his followers not to judge, he was making an important point and it's one we do well to listen to: I know my own heart, I'm not in a position any more than anyone else to lord it over anyone.

For us the egg is so scrambled, not only can you not see where the yellow and white bits begin and end, you may struggle to see where the toast and the plate begin and end too. Just when you think you have got it worked out, along comes a Bob, a Jenny or a Mary, a Lloyd or a Liz to mix it all up completely and redefine everything. Amid the chaos and the brokenness, the arms of Jesus reach out to us all regardless, and that tastes good. It doesn't always look pretty, but it tastes really good.

This continues to be the story of the gospel and the Christian community: personal and community transformation in intimate cohesion with each other and God. It is that image of Lloyd's window, one of complicated beauty and glorious chaos. We remain at home on the margins, but not content that life should stay the same for any of us.

13

Gethsemane

Despite the fact that my life is full of unpredictable people, chaos is not something I deliberately go looking for. But leadership seldom turns out the way you expect. Whether you are placed in a position of leadership, have risen through the ranks or whether others just gravitate towards you as guiding figure, you are probably there because you have a reputation for making good, wise choices along the way. Perhaps you have a productive track record that fits the ideals of the movement or organization and you are blessed with a natural dynamic, so people see something in you that they want to follow and learn from.

I've tried to do my best to make wise choices. Not in the first instance because I want to be a helpful leader, but because I really can't put up with the mess that poor choices result in. While I have a very cluttered desk and work space, I don't like a cluttered mind. I like to be able to think clearly and make well-thought-out reasoned judgements, but if I have to make a quick decision my gut instinct is usually one I am at peace with. I choose to be on good terms with people and work at relationships because I hate conflict; in fact I detest it. I try to live within my means because I don't like being in debt. I ride sensibly because I want my wife and children to have their husband and dad around. I choose not to get drunk because I want to be in control of my actions and I don't use amphetamine, cocaine or anything else because I dread to think what would happen if all this energy went in the wrong direction. In addition, I'm tired of burying friends in their thirties and forties. I see the chaos of poor choices all around me, while also being aware that many are not in a position of having alternative options available to them. Some are born into addiction, poverty, dysfunction, and starved of a stable environment, which leads to a survivalist, short-term decision-making existence. It's one that blocks out pain and the need to face demons head on, doing just what is necessary to get through each day.

The irony is, of course, that the more wisdom you appear to exhibit and the more people see you as someone who is reliable, steady and compassionate, the more likely they are to bring their chaos in your direction in the hope of finding some relief. In a life of shifting sands, any fixed anchor point of trust and source of support will be held on to tightly.

I didn't go looking for trouble, it found me. I did my best to make sensible choices that wouldn't bring disorder into my life, yet time and again I have found myself in the middle of someone else's troubles. As I reflect on nearly 30 years of ministry, nothing really prepares you for the onslaught of broken people. It is sometimes said that most of what a Christian minister does is absorb the pain of others. Sometimes there are mechanisms and structures to assist, but quite often you just keep soaking it up and eventually the sponge becomes full. The life of the minister, priest or pastor can be very isolating at times. You can leave yourself open, rather unwisely, to never being able to say no to a growing number of demands – taking another call, receiving another house guest, listening to another story, making another visit.

These days I can read the warning signs much better, but there was a time when I couldn't. Now I'll say no if I need to. I'm a people person, I thrive on human interaction, but I am also deeply introverted, so human interaction that is meaningful is also exhausting. I need recovery time and space to reflect and recharge. Now I understand the way I am wired and what I need to do to function amid the chaos.

Susan Cain's brilliant book *Quiet* was profoundly helpful in understanding what it is to live as an introvert in a world that can't stop talking. I only wish I had learned the lessons so much earlier. It becomes too easy to think that everyone wants a piece of you and with our high-tech constant communication methods, it is now possible to be accessible all of the time to everyone, if you allow yourself to be. Even if you don't reply to a message immediately, the sender will know that you have read it, or are online, and wonder why you can't respond straight away, but 24-hour accessibility should not necessarily mean 24-hour availability. For the introvert, the constant bombardment of human connection can be very draining.

My darkest places are when I have felt as if I have absolutely nothing more left to give, when I have been ground down to the point of exhaustion. You put yourself out there, and for as long as you are visible and accessible, you are available as a listening ear, someone to offer a word of advice or share a burden. At its most extreme it feels like my flesh has been pecked away at by hungry birds. 'Can I have a word? Have you got five minutes? What are you doing tomorrow? Can you, can you, can you . . . ?' Human heartaches, questions and demands, stack up one on top the other. Eventually with the constant pecking, the nerve ends start to fray. The cocktail of demands, pressures and responsibilities from all aspects of your life cause the sponge to be saturated. You are being pulled in ten different directions. You think you are going mad. In isolation you try to find a way through, but it's like running in treacle or trying to stir a bucket of bricks with a pencil. At its worst, it becomes an intolerable burden and is indeed a very dark place to be.

At one point, after a particular series of events, I really thought I had got to the end of the road. In addition to regular family, Zac's Place and God's Squad responsibilities, several very complex pastoral issues were going on, including a real betrayal of trust. I was also regularly receiving disturbing calls in the early hours of the morning from a friend with serious mental health issues. I was caught up in a conflict between two motorcycle clubs that had all the potential for turning nasty, there was illness at home, and we had numerous overseas house guests lined up to come and stay. We also received news about losing significant financial assistance at a time when our support structures were shaky anyway. But on the surface, everything was going brilliantly! It really was an incredibly creative, deeply moving and productive time of ministry, but I felt I was going under.

Even the simplest of tasks seemed to be an intolerable burden and eventually I was reduced to an exhausted wreck with simply no more to give. The accumulation of other people's pain, confusion, anger, hatred, aggression and needs became too much. My thoughts went places I didn't want them to go; I muddled through options in blinks of an eye, until eventually I came to that moment of surrender, a returning to poverty of spirit, an emptying as the sponge is wrung out. In fragile moments of darkness, I dared to utter the words of Christ, 'Not my will, but yours be done', and with faith held together by sinews stretched to the limit I hoped God would give me the strength to carry on.

These moments become my Gethsemane. Gethsemane was the garden Jesus retreated to and it was the place of his darkest hour prior to his crucifixion. He waited long into the night for his betrayer's kiss, and as his friends slept he sweated over the road of attrition that lay ahead. Of course, he was familiar with the physical torture and pain that was to come. Roman crucifixions were commonplace around Jerusalem. But as he ran through all that lay ahead, it wasn't the agonizing physical torture that he feared the most. It was the pain of separation from the Father that weighed heaviest.

The burden of redemption responsibility almost seemed a bridge too far. 'Is this a road I have to go down? Is there another way? Is this a cup of suffering and separation I really have to drink from?' These were very real questions that Jesus was wrestling with. I believe he entered an unbelievably dark place, almost beyond comprehension. If I am to believe that he was tempted in every way, he will have considered all his options at this point. If we are to find in Christ anything that identifies with dark depression, the torment of mental illness, burnout, suicidal thoughts – or simply choosing to bail out and set up home with Mary as the film *The Last Temptation of Christ* suggests – it is in the garden of Gethsemane.

The anguish of the Psalms of David, the Laments of Jeremiah, the torture of Job – the whole range of darkest human experiences stared Jesus down. The anguish and tears in the eyes of the victims of abuse, rape, racism, hatred; the confusion of mental health and the prison of addiction; the scourge of slavery, genocide and domestic violence, and so the list goes on. Sweat like drops of blood carried the tears of the brokenhearted as the cup of suffering flowed over.

If we are to follow the way of Christ, to take up our cross as he taught his friends, we will at some stage travel through Gethsemane. We might even visit it regularly. Be careful: it isn't where you want to set up home, but as we pass through we take the disturbing path of Gethsemane with Christ. In Gethsemane, Jesus considered his options; he didn't avoid the issues and he chose to drink that cup of suffering. As his journey continued, via kangaroo courts and brutal beatings, to an out-of-town rubbish dump littered with human remains, I am sure he reflected on his sleeping disciples now way off in the shadows, nowhere to be seen. He'd tasted Judas' bittersweet kiss. The crowd that cheered as he entered Jerusalem now jeered for his death. The Pharisees had the facts in front of them but nothing connected in their hearts. Enthusiastic Peter typically drawing his sword in the garden then denied even knowing him. It was a repeating pattern. In his nakedness as he saw his clothes being divided among his aggressors, everything within him could have said, 'That's it, you bunch of bastards, just piss off and leave me here to die, won't you?' He could have, but he didn't. Instead he uttered words of redemption not condemnation: 'Father, forgive them. They don't know what they are doing.' The gospel of Jesus of Nazareth is both mysterious and traumatic. It needed to be. Gethsemane is a place of uncertainty, of struggle and confusion. It is that place where dark moments of doubt are framed in fear and betrayal. Gethsemane is the place I have come to visit, sit with my exhaustion and wrestle with my questions, doubts and fears.

Andy desperately wanted to be part of God's Squad. His initial conversion to the Christian faith had been quite dramatic. While he was in a psychotic frenzy in the middle of a thunderstorm, a poster on a church noticeboard caught his attention. He ripped it from the board and in the following days started to explore what the verses of Scripture might mean. He was frequently erratic in his behaviour, requiring a cocktail of prescription medication for mental health stability, but chronic alcoholism often nullified their effects. Hospitalization, arrests, secure mental health units, the pit of despair and driving bans were a regular cycle. While his life was too chaotic for him to be a God's Squad member, Andy found in us a community to be part of and as time went on his life stabilized. His friendship was fiercely loyal and he was a sensitive and talented artist. On a good day he was incredibly industrious, almost to the point of manic. He would often produce a piece of work as a gift and in his brokenness his fragile faith radiated rainbows of peace against a dark sky.

For Andy that dark sky was a brutal story of sexual abuse from his time in boarding school. Such was the weight of fear he carried for nearly 40 years, it was not until his abusers were brought to trial that he discovered that his own brother had also suffered similar abuse. Andy didn't live to see the guilty verdict, though. Like so many others, the pain and torment had become too much. His whole life had been invaded by an imposter he could not shake off. One day he went into his shed, strung himself up and kicked the box away.

I know that Andy is now free of all that held him captive, but the burden still weighs heavy for us who remain. The missed last call moments before he took that final walk. Could we have done more? What do you do with a burden like this? After Andy's funeral, his brother gave us a large old wooden crucifix, which he had distressed with additional wear and tear, the original shine now significantly diminished and tarnished. The added scuffs and scrapes somehow seemed like poignant question marks to unanswerable questions.

When Jayne's brother Chris died in a car accident just before we got married, nothing made sense. Nothing ever does in these circumstances. A young man, enthusiastic in his faith and all that life was to bring, gone without warning. All of a sudden, a family is thrown into complete turmoil. In these circumstances some people you think will come good have no idea what to do or say, and disappear, whereas people you never expected to be there come good – but some won't go away. True loyalty and friendship comes to the fore, as an emotional freefall makes you feel sicker than you ever thought possible. What was a stable faith gets shaky.

In reality, for all the rhetoric, we discovered that the more conventional expressions of church, which both Jayne and I experienced growing up, often have little idea how to deal with death. Alongside beautiful, sustaining acts of kindness are words aplenty of resurrection, affirmation and the hope of the eternal. But they just ring hollow when you are in Gethsemane. When you feel as if someone has reached inside your core and pulled your very soul out, no words, prayers, pious platitudes, rousing Welsh hymns or evangelical grins can begin to bathe the wounds of the most traumatic grief at its most raw.

It's only now, many years on, that I can see how deep an impact the sudden death of Jayne's brother had on me, not just in terms of personal loss but in understanding how inadequate the Church can be in dealing with grief, and how more broadly in our society we try to navigate a path that ignores the reality of death. We can all too easily end up with a very shallow theology of pain and suffering. We are almost embarrassed by death and may reflect our broader Western cultural conditioning by living in denial of it. It's a weakness we dare not show, lest we reveal any sign of defeat or lack of faith. Woe betide the person who dares to ask questions of God.

Somehow, by saying and believing, which I do with all my heart, that 'death is not the end' and we shall know reunion with those who've gone before, we are able to navigate around the rawness and questions of grief.

When we are alongside those in grief and the temptation is there to start preaching, we need to learn to keep our mouths shut and just walk with those who are suffering, in silence if necessary. Sometimes there are no appropriate words pastorally. We may need to give room for those in trauma to use lots of inappropriate words and we have to listen, not 'tut' and have concerns about them losing their faith because they've used a naughty word. Finding the language and a secure place to express it in the face of pain and loss is a choice that people are often denied, but it is essential to create such places without shame or fear.

Let us celebrate the hope of Christ and the resurrection of our weary bodies, but not at the expense of allowing a wound to bleed a while, of allowing the blues to be sung and grief shared, or of allowing the scar to form and serve as a reminder of the pain, and maybe also then a reminder of God's merciful comfort. I am tired of attending funerals, particularly evangelical ones, where you are made to feel guilty for feeling sorrow and mourning. I don't like it when funerals – and weddings, for that matter – are hijacked as a platform to preach a 'turn or burn' sermon. The sudden and untimely death of a loved one changes normality for ever in a family. This cannot be glossed over, erased or ignored. One reason the Church sometimes fails to connect with people is because we are not honest enough in our relationships with the questions we carry. Until we encourage a way of being comfortable travelling companions with pain, questions, doubts, fears and grief, we will always be short-changing ourselves and the communities we serve of the greater hope we carry within. None of us is immune to Gethsemane struggles.

A friend and staunch advocate of the support we give at Zac's Place, Steve Balsamo, sang the lead in Andrew Lloyd Webber's *Jesus Christ Superstar* in London's West End in the 1990s. His version of the song 'Gethsemane' still stands out as one of the best performances in all the productions of that musical. The song and Steve's recordings of it brilliantly capture the tension and the struggle of Christ in the garden. It really is remarkable. In my mind, when you add the Gethsemane imagery of Mel Gibson's film *The Passion* to the mix, which has the devil portrayed hovering and brooding in the garden shadows, waiting to snatch and steal, we find creative layers that help us understand these moments when Jesus plumbed the depths of despair and questioned his reasons for taking the way of the cross. To enter into the heart of Christ in Gethsemane is to allow Christ to enter into our darkness, our isolation, our moments of imminent pain – times when there seem to be no guarantees that everything is going to be OK.

Of all the decisions I have made in my life, choosing the way of Christ has been the wisest by a very big margin. It has coloured just about every other decision that has followed and has been the decisive factor in whether to give up or hold on. Ultimately Gethsemane and the cross was followed by the resurrection. Learning to live between a full revelation of the cross and the resurrection enables me to get through my Gethsemanes. It is as if Gethsemane lies at the midpoint of each of the Beatitudes – that moment of suspension between knowing what the promise says and what the present reality feels like.

After a series of studies in the Old Testament book of Lamentations in our regular Zac's Place gatherings, we explored the idea of finding a language for our own pain and suffering. Around 30 of our incredibly diverse Zac's Place community contributed in writing the following lament.[5]

A Zac's Place lament

God, I feel worn out, frustrated.
I am too busy being busy to notice what people need,
yet I judge them because I feel I am the one who has to
do all the work.
I am a let-down, embarrassed at the state I sometimes
find myself in and crushed when those close to me see
me like that.
My heart is heavy because my words have caused hurt
to others;
I have brought disharmony to my family.
My parents have seen their hopes fade and they – and I –
have seen the effects of addiction on those we love.
I see those who suffer from illness and those who mourn
with grief so deep at the loss of their parents.
And with eyes that can no longer cry I give the word for
my beautiful dog to be put to sleep.
My stupidity, naivety, fear and anxiety get in the way
and stop me helping others.
I've been taking God for granted,
missing out on the freshness of his love.
I wish time could be reversed; what if I had done things
differently?

The city has a heavy spirit of despair, where is hope?
It has never recovered from past hurts;
many great shops have closed down
and money has been wasted on foolish projects.
Greed and materialism have taken up residence.
We've given up on our dreams and our passions.

Nobody cares about our environment or government,
because we believe we are powerless to change
anything.
We experience a lack of community, concern and love
where the homeless are treated like nobodies,
people are rejected instead of embraced
and a huge amount of food is wasted.
An offer of friendship is seen as weakness
and there is no appreciation for those who help others.
Only the gossips, who find pleasure in reminding us
of our past failings, thrive.

The world is round like the lives people lead, always
coming back to the same conclusion:
Where is hope?
We have the society we deserve, a throwaway society
where racism, violence and rubbish abound, where it's
every man for himself. Self, self, self.
Governments everywhere act out of selfish interests
instead of for the common good.
Migrants, child soldiers, Syria, cruelty to animals, torture,
rape, degradation of women, Palestine, injustice, fear,
refugees, hatred, sorrow.
We have lost our passion for justice; we have lost respect
for all living creatures.
Where is hope?

All who hope make hope.
Hope is finding a purpose, putting an idea in place when
there is nothing left to salvage – and believing that it will
come to pass.
Hope is in places like Zac's where people talk to each
other and treat each other with respect.
Hope is in drug agencies and churches beginning to
work together for people instead of preaching at them.
Hope is seen in surprising places, in street children who
should have none.

Hope is in people who care, people like us, people
who will work 100% for God.
I believe God has a wider plan,
one that will use people's gifts to help put things right,
one that through prayer, community and action will
produce fruit.
When we love each other, when we allow ourselves to
be the wild sacred beings God created,
we are powerful beyond measure.
With God's help
we can be the change we want to see in the world.
God's love and grace are overwhelming,
his forgiveness never-ending.

14

Interruptions and side tracks

One of the pleasures in choosing to ride a motorcycle is that the journey itself can become an adventure. The events that happen between point A and point B can become as significant as the reason for the road trip in the first place, as interruptions and interactions en route colour the experience. Admittedly they are not always welcome interruptions, such as a storm, a breakdown or an accident, but on the whole every biker will enjoy a road trip. Journeys continue to be opportunity for ongoing discovery, new experiences and nurturing a steadfast commitment to stay the course in tough conditions. Knowing what the destination will bring can give us focus, even when there is no guarantee of what lies between the now and our final resting place.

Jesus' friends travelled with him on the road, a band of unlikely travellers if ever there was. They lived simply, learned to love extravagantly, failed miserably at times, experienced a kaleidoscope of emotions; laughter, tears, tensions, heartache and questions all coloured that experience. Crucially, though, these followers learned from the master as they went along. They watched, and they listened to soundbites of instruction that were robustly demonstrated with integrity by their leader. Jesus calls us to live and engage with the world with our eyes open, but too often the learning experience offered by the Church to would-be disciples is disengaged from the interruptions, delays and side tracks of the road. It can be tempting to opt for the comfort of an insulated ghetto.

I find the resurrection narrative in the Gospels compelling and fascinating. Here the disciples think the road trip has come to an end. Their journey is done. Their leader is dead. Any words of promised resurrection have soon been forgotten and the miraculous encounters of the past mean nothing any more as fear sets in. Jesus is dead. What is more, they discover that his body is no longer in the grave. When considering an alternative narrative to the story at this point, I assume that having been resurrected, Jesus could have stayed in the tomb. The women who arrived at the tomb, followed by the male members of the community that made up Jesus' followers, could have found Jesus inside, sitting on the stone slab next to a pile of neatly folded linen cloth, with a kind of 'What time do you call this?' look about his face.

There is Jesus, very much alive, but still sitting in the tomb waiting for the world to walk in. This has been my experience of many church communities. We profess faith, maybe even a radical transformational faith, but we still hang on to the comfort of staying within the safety of the tomb. 'Why do you look for the living among the dead?' Indeed! The resurrection took place because the journey had not ended. The destination is clear but the adventure continues outside of the grave, without the baggage of our grave clothes. The followers of Jesus are not encouraged to peer at the world through the entrance of a grave, but to live life fully, amid the muck and the mire, the laughter and the tears, the joy and the pain.

Over the years, especially when I was leading God's Squad into Europe and also through opportunities to travel and minister in other places, I have learned not only to enjoy the epic road trips, both in a pack of club mates and the solo journeys, but to embrace the diversions that happen along the way. These interruptions, delays, wrong turns and extra encounters can happen when you are way too exhausted to think you care. I offer these anecdotes as postcards, if you like, from foreign lands and from home, with an invitation and a challenge of 'Wish you were here', either to stand alongside and help or to breathe deeply and see something beautiful.

Ukraine

I first arrived in Kiev, Ukraine in a thunderstorm of epic proportions. I saw more accidents on the flooded excuse for a freeway in the short distance from the city airport to the block of flats where I was staying for the night than in the past few years put together. It was my first visit and as with all such trips, you greet a host of alternative sounds, smells, tastes and interactions with both caution and anticipation. To this day I have no idea where the empty flat was I stayed in, or whose it was – there is always an element of trust involved – but I do remember looking out of the window in the morning to see a car submerged in the flooded street, such was the extent of the rain.

It was to be a relatively straightforward visit. We had contacts in Ukraine who wanted to explore the process for starting a chapter of God's Squad. I was to spend some time with all those interested, ride with them to a motorcycle event, get a feel for how they interacted with the clubs and also engage the clubs there in some early dialogue. Bearing in mind I speak no Ukrainian or Russian, I had to rely completely on Pasha's basic English for translation.

The bike show went well and I was received warmly as the first ever overseas visitor to the event. I was invited to present the winners' trophies and speak about God's Squad's mission. It was a real throwback to the 1970s for me to see so many radical back-yard modified bikes with extreme handlebars and kicked-out front wheels. The bike culture was alive and well in Ukraine, but it felt like a different decade in respect of engineering! We were getting ready to leave the event when one of the members from a club present asked if I would like to travel with him to see where he grew up. Time was tight and I could sense my hosts were keen to get away, but we took up the invitation and all travelled from the event site. Again, I have no recollection of where, but I do remember this biker's face as we sat and talked amid the remains of the orphanage where he had grown up.

His skin was scarred, almost as if it had been burned, and for an hour he recounted his life story of growing up in the shadow of Chernobyl and living with the legacy of the nuclear disaster. He spoke of his own physical pain, the premature loss of loved ones and the physical deformities that afflict so many in his community. He spoke of the anger he feels at the one penny a day compensation he and others get from the government as scant recognition for the trauma, pain and heartache. He spoke of the sorrow he feels that he has never had an opportunity to tell anyone of his heartache, because nobody he knows can do anything. He spoke of the isolation, of what it feels like to be a forgotten people. Afterwards, with tears in his eyes, he said, 'Thank you for listening. I have never had anyone to tell this to before. Thank you for visiting; please tell your people we are still here.' In broken English, hand signals and facial expressions we connected, and a story was shared and both our lives were richer for it. Twelve years on, I owe it to this biker and his people to remind the world that the legacy and the children of Chernobyl are still there in a seldom visited cul-de-sac.

The second interruption of this road trip was nothing short of a catastrophe. It was late into the night as we headed out of the area. I was now travelling with Pasha in the front seat of his car, and his young wife and infant son were in the rear seat. Others were taking the bikes and I had given Sasha, who was riding immediately behind us, my heavy-duty waterproof protective jacket as the temperature had dropped considerably. Sasha's headlight was ever present in the rear window as Pasha and I talked about the day's events.

Out of nowhere, a car veered towards us out of the pitch-black night. The huge old Ukrainian saloon had no headlights on. We swerved and just managed to avoid a head-on collision. As we straightened up and breathed a sigh of relief, we realized that Sasha's headlight had vanished; he was no longer there. We stopped, turned the car around and crawled along slowly until we saw the form of a person at the side of the road and the wreckage of a bike. Further down the ravine the other driver was trying to restart his engine to make his escape. Getting out of the car, we could hear Sasha's eerie semi-conscious moans and could smell the spilled fuel.

The hunk of steel had hit Sasha's left-hand side. His left arm had a serious injury and he was in shock needing urgent medical attention, far beyond any first aid I could administer. We were in a rural community, and the night had become dawn by the time Sasha was taken to hospital in what looked like an old post office van from the 1960s, with a deck chair in the back and a blue light that glimmered every 30 seconds.

While Sasha was being treated, I was held in a local police interview room with an exceedingly drunk local man protesting his innocence, having nearly killed my new friend. It was disorienting and a long night of mixed emotions. Sasha never got either adequate medical treatment for his injuries from the state healthcare system or justice from the courts. Friendships forged on the road are some of the best, and this long night created a bond that would become significant in the development of the Ukrainian chapter of God's Squad some years later.

The third interruption of that short visit to Ukraine, which also included a long return road trip south to Odessa, was an off-chance visit to the home of a couple named Bogdan and Anya in Kiev. Bogdan and his friend Sergey were keen bikers, and also Christians. Pasha thought it might be worth calling in to meet them. But it wasn't the workshop full of old bikes and engineering equipment that made an impact on me, it was their kitchen. As I sat in Bogdan and Anya's kitchen drinking coffee with them, I became aware of a constant stream of teenagers in and out of the kitchen and living area. Some were chilling out, others were working through a list of chores and some who were studying English were keen to try it out on the visitor. I was in a family kitchen, but it was more than that.

It transpired that Bogdan and Anya had begun, probably in their late twenties, to care for teenagers who had come to the end of their time in state-run orphanages. Many of these children were from traumatized backgrounds, some had parents in prison or had chronic addictions to alcohol or drugs. On leaving the state orphanages with virtually no education, most of the boys would be likely to end up in prison and many of the girls would be pulled into the sex trade. But here was this young, committed Christian couple prepared to open up their home and their lives to give some of these teenagers an alternative. And not just their home; they made a way to open up their family and formally adopt the young people.

Many of these young people subsequently gained access to college and work and, more importantly, they came to know the embrace of a family. Through the love and care of a functional family they were able to break the cycle of trauma and pain that saw them rejected as children. I was in the kitchen of a home that is called Safe Haven. It remains my favourite kitchen anywhere in the world, after my own, and whenever I am in Kiev it also becomes my safe haven as I catch up with an ever-increasing number of family stories. By now, Bogdan and Anya must be the proud parents of over a hundred adopted children as well as their own young boys.

I have travelled to the Ukraine on numerous occasions, each time with an agenda to give something by way of teaching, encouragement or guidance. I have come away from every visit enriched, having been in the company of some of the most resilient, resourceful, beautiful people. Some interruptions to the schedule frustrate us, some traumatize us and some warm our hearts beyond measure. But they all have the capacity to transform us one way or another.

Australia

Trips to Australia as the founding land of God's Squad have been frequent over the years. Initially they were journeys I would undertake to learn from experienced members of the club there and gain wisdom. As the years have gone by and during my tenure as both European President and International Vice President, the trips have become more about me having something to contribute to the club and church communities there, rather than feeding my own soul. If there was a pivotal point of change in emphasis it would have been when I was ordained at St Martin's in Collingwood, Melbourne in 2002, which was the spiritual home of God's Squad.

The trips have also brought opportunities to minister widely in various contexts. I have often been able to arrange additional speaking engagements on the road to make maximum use of the time and expense of getting there. In 2009 I undertook a short speaking tour after I had contributed teaching at the God's Squad national run in Launceston, Tasmania. Smithy was completing his doctorate in the USA and I deputized at his request, bringing some Bible teaching for the Australian membership. After the weekend's retreat, I embarked on a series of dates from Melbourne in Victoria in the south-east and up the east coast to Brisbane in Queensland. A different town each day, taking on engagements at Glenrowan, Canberra, Sydney, Newcastle and Lismore. The ever generous Magoo in Melbourne loaned me his Harley Evolution Softail, which he had just renovated, and I travelled to speak in various churches, support local God's Squad chapters with club visits and encourage our families as I stayed with them.

By this time Glenn and Ros, who had spent a few years with us in Swansea, had returned to Canberra and were embarking on the early stages of developing a Zac's Place mission community in the small country town of Yass. I met up with Glenn in a place called Gundagai. Here we parked the bikes and marvelled at the huge old wooden bridge that spanned a very parched flood plain of the Murrumbidgee river in the heart of the town. This bridge prompted some investigative work on Glenn's part and we learned that the flood plain had been the place of an incredible act of heroism by two local Aboriginal men, Yarri and Jacky Jacky in 1852. For as long as the white men had turned up and started to build their houses, the original and first land occupiers there told them, 'Don't build your homes there, it's a flood plain.' The stories they had passed down through generations included warnings that this river would one day return and fill the plain. In a typically dismissive response, the immigrant settlers continued to build, ignoring the wisdom of the native people. Finally, the days came when the rain did not stop. The flood plain was filled with a raging river for days on end. Having stood on the bed of the dry plain, it is hard to imagine it full, but the natural awesome strength of the water must have been petrifyingly intimidating to anyone within reach.

Despite the strength of the currents, a local man, Yarri, entered the river in a simple dugout canoe. Battling against the rising waters, he rescued scores of people. He was later joined by Jacky Jacky, who added to those saved, as the two men paddled on the rim of survival and death. Not only was this a colossal act of heroic bravery, it inverted the social structure of what the white man had brought into that community. The Aboriginal people were abused and treated as slaves, their opinions did not count, their voices were not listened to. Yet it was these two ostracized men who were prepared to enter the turbulent middle ground of racial and cultural tension and do the right thing on a bad day. Their character, their virtue, hung on a spine that leapt into action regardless of what resentment they may have held towards the white oppressors. They acted. They made a difference.

This is widely thought to be one of the first acts of reconciliation between the original owners of the land and the settlers. I find it poignant that it was the oppressed and marginalized community that took that step into the dangerous middle ground. They could have gloated at the settlers' folly, but Yarri and Jacky Jacky showed a strength of character and depth of integrity that challenged the expected patterns of behaviour. Over one third of the town's population died in those floods, but almost as many more were pulled into bark canoes and led to safety. These two men chose to extend a saving embrace towards those who had not necessarily shown them favour.

In honour of this deeply righteous act, this story is captured in a beautiful painting commissioned as part of our Zac's Place Beatitudes art project, using a fusion of traditional Aboriginal and contemporary ideas by Canberra-based artist Yidinji. Quite rightly it offers a reflection on Jesus' words, 'Blessed are the peacemakers, for they will be called children of God.'

These heroic acts were also eventually acknowledged by later generations of the local community. In recent years a statue has been placed in the community, but by and large this had been a lost story. The irony is that just a few miles away near the freeway there sits another monument called The Dog on the Tuckerbox, which celebrates early pioneer settlers, where tourists stop and have their photos taken. Crowds are not always drawn to what feeds the soul the most and this is certainly the case here.

So looking in awe at the engineering excellence of an old bridge led to a fascination with a story of reconciliation and a piece of Aboriginal work that now hangs at Zac's Place in Swansea. I carried that story with me up the east coast, taking the opportunity of educating the present settlers about the untaught history of the land that has brought them so much privilege.

Continuing north from southern New South Wales and on to Sydney, I entered a city that was awash with news channel reports on motorcycle clubs because of a recent conflict. I engaged with the dialogue our members were having there in bringing reconciliation with the region's clubs and saw first hand the progress that was taking place. The following day I exited the city over the famous bridge and continued north to Newcastle. On most of that road trip I was accompanied by another God's Squad member from whichever local chapter I was passing through. That's how you get to hear about the local stories and history; it is also safe practice, especially if you are travelling through the bush and small country towns. Kangaroos are unpredictable creatures and are the cause of many road deaths, so having a source of local knowledge with you on the road can be a help, especially at dawn and dusk. Some days, though, it's good to be alone and have some head-space to yourself. The leg from Newcastle, where I had spoken in a church and caught up with friends, up to Coffs Harbour provided that opportunity.

In searing heat of around 40 degrees, I steadily clocked the kilometres up on the freeway, the Harley reliably thumping along its regular beat. At some point on the ride I had one of those sensations when you feel that someone is watching you. I checked the mirrors; I hadn't seen another vehicle for at least half an hour, there were no police cars behind or speed traps ahead to be worried about. Then I looked to my right. Just a few metres away, a wedge-tailed eagle was cruising alongside me, majestically gliding along at a steady 110 kilometres an hour. Then it soared back towards the heavens to cast its eyes on something more appetizing.

Moments like this on the road help you forget the rides back home in winter, body screaming with pain with fingers so cold, it's ten below zero and you still have 100 miles to go and the only thing flying through the air is a wayward ratchet strap from a truck. Having said that, you tend not to get the stench of a rotting kangaroo carcass or a rogue brown snake at the side of the M4 motorway. My journey ended that night in the company of the God's Squad community in Lismore, sharing a meal with the local Aboriginal community. Here I was honoured to receive the traditional Welcome to Country from local Bundjalung elder Aunty Dorrie, a truly remarkable lady in many ways, not least as she was the first ordained Aboriginal woman in the Uniting Church in Australia.

For me, the road remains not just a means to get somewhere but an ongoing opportunity to live with eyes wide open and embrace what happens on the periphery so easily overlooked. Sometimes in our haste to reach our final destinations, we pass by poignant stories rich in culture and history, we don't see the beauty of the natural world and we can miss the milestone markers of God's grace along the way.

New Zealand – Aotearoa

I arrived at Auckland airport to be questioned by a rather sarcastic immigration officer who was struggling to see why an Anglican bishop had invited a weary-looking middle-aged biker to conduct a series of meetings in New Zealand. In good God's Squad fashion, the chapter there had organized a bike for me. Our New Zealand President, Buckshot, who is also an Anglican priest, met me at the airport and along with Al, another God's Squad member, we headed to a local clubhouse before my first speaking engagement of what became an incredible 13-day tour that snaked from almost the top of the north island down its entire length, finishing in Wellington. Venues were as diverse as you could get: the cathedral in Hamilton, pizza restaurants, theology colleges, a festival and numerous church communities.

Memorable experiences include wonderful engagement with a Catholic worker community family in the far north who were fighting a court battle with the US government over the disabling of US military equipment on New Zealand soil which had contributed to the death of civilians overseas. On the road, we were pulled over by the police three times for no reason other than wearing our colours. I received beautiful Maori welcomes and hospitality in homes and at their *marae* (Maori sacred spaces), thanks largely to Buckshot's hard-earned respect and commitment to his nation's indigenous people. In between venues, we took the opportunity to swim in Lake Taupo and on the way rather bizarrely we kept bumping into people I knew. Turning up at the Harley dealership in Auckland to get a puncture fixed, I was greeted with, 'Hello, Sean, what are you doing here?' It was the last thing I expected! There were bike shows and the obligatory clubhouses to visit along the way as we rode through some of the most spectacular scenery imaginable. Meetings in a host of different venues went well; I was truly humbled by both the welcome and how receptive people everywhere were to the stories from Zac's Place and my encouragement to embrace Jesus' teaching and example in mission-shaped church. The road delivered, as it always does, a rich variety of encounters and experiences. None more so than at the grave of a 12-year-old girl who had died in 1836.

Buckshot knew that this grave existed somewhere near the country town of Matamata. We searched up and down this single-track lane over and over, until eventually we spotted a stone marker with an inscription and this led to a dry, rutted dirt track across a field. The four of us rode across the field, kicking up a huge plume of dust, though respectfully we shut the engines off as we sighted the simple grave, marked with a white wooden cross and surrounded by a low white picket fence. Thick road dirt on our faces, we four grubby bikers silently walked towards the grave and read the simple plaque. We then sat in silence for possibly 30 minutes before reflecting and praying together on what these moments had brought.

Tarore was the daughter of a Maori chief. She had been given a copy of Luke's Gospel in *te reo Maori* (the Maori language) by her teacher at the mission school she attended. It was a gift she grew to treasure and she carried it constantly in a flax bag worn around her neck. While she was camping with some of her tribe, a neighbouring hostile tribe raided them in the middle of the night, stealing what they could. As Tarore slept, she received a blow to her head and died. Thinking that the flax bag necklace might be of some value, her killer ripped it from her neck, taking it as a trophy.

There was popular desire for revenge, or *utu* in Maori, but at her funeral Tarore's father Ngakuko spoke against any traditional and expected reprisal, stating that the tribal warfare had already caused too much pain and bloodshed. In his grief, he challenged his people to trust in the justice of God and not the traditional act of *utu*. Once again it took the courage of a broken man who was brave enough to resolve to do things differently to show a different way.

Eventually the invading tribe came to hear what was in the Gospel of Luke that had been stolen from Tarore, via a visiting slave who was literate enough to read the text. Tarore's murderer, Uita, was deeply convicted by what he heard, and responded by seeking forgiveness from Tarore's father. A risky move in any culture at any time – this could easily have resulted in his own death, but it didn't. Instead, as the two men tearfully embraced it signalled the end of the warfare between the tribes, and not just in this region but eventually throughout the whole of the north and south islands. Tarore's Luke's Gospel was read across the land. The plaque on her grave simply states that her death brought peace to the tribes.

Sometimes the road brings a defining story that leaves you reeling in the mystery of all that is despicable and all that is wondrous in the whole of human experience – a mystery that dares to allow the threads of God's grace to weave its colour on to a dark canvas. I can't fully explain what happened as we sat in the dry grass alongside Tarore's grave. I know it challenged us, it moved us. Of all the roadside interruptions and detours, I shall never forget that sacred moment when we were reminded of the impact of the gospel, the good news, on a community at war, the fragility of a young girl, and the brokenness of warrior chiefs. How we need the faith of a Tarore, the courage of her father Ngakuko and the embrace of both him and Tarore's killer, Uita, in our world of conflict. I wish you were here. I wish we were all there.

Michigan, USA

I have a love–hate relationship with the United States. I have fond memories of living in Virginia as a child, but am so glad we never stayed. The music in my ears comes from many American songwriters: Springsteen, Mellencamp, Petty, Cash and Dylan to name just a few. I ride a Harley Davidson not because it's American but because it's reliable, economical, holds its resale value well and is an enjoyable challenge to ride. There are not many older vehicles you can do 100,000 miles on and sell for just £1,000 less than you paid for it. But some things about America don't add up as well as the resale of a Harley. This was epitomized on a visit to Michigan exploring options for setting up a God's Squad chapter there.

It was 4 July, Independence Day weekend, and my host Tom, who became our founding president there, was helping out at a large community barbecue in his town for the homeless and those who were struggling to make ends meet. He and his wife Janice were already committed to feeding people who would gather at night at the bus station in their neighbourhood, but this was on a different scale. I have never seen both a grill and a food queue so huge! Tom and others worked heroically all day in the heat of both the sun and the grill fire, catering for several hundred people cooking racks of ribs, steaks and chicken.

At the beginning of the meal, while everyone was patiently waiting in line, the hosting minister got everyone's attention then led us in a prayer of thanks for the food. Just across town an air show was happening for those with tickets, who weren't relying on a free meal. As the Blue Angels display team flew overhead, the community meal host celebrated their arrival and asked how many of those in the line for food were military veterans. 'Hands up if you are proud to be a veteran!' she exclaimed. About 50 per cent of them put their hands up. These folks living under bridges or in the bus station, with ailments and injuries they could not afford to get treated, were proud soldiers, some fighting flashbacks that they tried to numb with alcohol. These men and women, who had put their hand up for their country, were now putting their hands out for food, as the aviation fuel burned above our heads.

The following day I had an almost catastrophic mechanical failure on the bike while riding to Hell and back, as a series of bolts worked loose on the rear pulley of the bike I was borrowing, almost causing the rear wheel to seize. (Yes, there is a town in Michigan called Hell, and yes, there's a motorcycle club with a bottom rocker stating Hell. I'm not sure if there's such thing as Hell parish church, though. I didn't stay for long enough to find out – it was too hot.)

Prior to this short excursion I had been sitting in the back row of a small-town Wesleyan Methodist Chapel, and unexpectedly invited to preach at the service there by the gentle and generous minister who extended a welcome to this stranger in town.

Whatever the contradictions, there are glimmers of the eternal in the lives of Tom and the other volunteers serving without prejudice, and in the welcome of a small-town minister faithfully serving his parish.

However long the queue for food in Michigan was, back home in Swansea there was one man who wouldn't be seen dead joining the food queue.

Swansea, Wales

As I put the key into the lock to bring the roller shutter down in front of the red door, a shuffling, hunched figure, dragging his bag up the lane behind him, was stoically emerging from the misty shadows of the Swansea night. There was only one man this silhouette could belong to – worn-out ill-fitting boots, baggy trousers with the legs stuffed full, a long wax jacket and a large floppy woolly hat atop a long mane of matted dreads.

Pete had been waiting just out of sight for the Zac's Place gathering to finish, to catch me for our regular Tuesday night chat. I held out my hand and shook his, which was clothed in a very soggy, rancid, woollen fingerless glove. As usual his jacket was unbuttoned, his matted fleece pullover was unzipped and what looked like a black T-shirt underneath was actually his grubby skin. 'Hello, Pete. What's new?' I asked, knowing that we would spend somewhere between one and two hours standing in the rain, putting the world to rights. Pete would do most of the talking, pausing only into silence as a passer-by strolled past. They might utter, 'Alright, Pete,' and give him a respectful nod. Pete would nod back but have a resigned look of indignation that someone had dared to walk through what was essentially his front room, albeit a public footpath, and disturb his conversation.

Pete was something of a local treasure and an enigma in equal measure. He had been sleeping rough for as long as anyone could remember, certainly over 30 years. He was one of those characters everybody saw and thought they knew because he'd always been there. He sat in the square surrounded by his bags, surveying the scene, watching, always watching. Going about his daily routine, he took everything in, fascinated by people's patterns of behaviour as he absorbed the rhythms of city life in Swansea. The poor daytime drunks sitting in the square, the wealthy night-time drunks letting off steam, those who would catch his eye while shopping, those who would stop for a chat, those who would hastily move on and those who were in his 'top ten'. Pete had learned to rely and depend on a small select band of friends over the years, from whom he would accept help, and these were his top ten. As he got older and people moved on, or died, his top ten gradually reduced in number and he became more dependent on just a handful of trusted friends, and this troubled him.

He saw life differently from most people. He had never known his natural father, and he and his mother relocated from the West Country to Swansea when he was an infant. Having grown up in poverty, by the time he was 26 he had also lost his stepfather and his younger brother, who had died in a freak accident. Pete was fiercely independent, with an incredible intellect, and somewhere along the way, for reasons only known to him, he had chosen to live an alternative lifestyle on the streets. People find themselves homeless for all manner of reasons and there are caring people who work tirelessly to meet their needs in most communities. Swansea is no exception, but Pete was a mystery to just about everyone within the circle of official support networks. Knowing that I had a good relationship with Pete, those who could make things happen in the city would ask, 'What can we do for Pete?' Many options were considered, but they were never a match for his very particular criteria. He would say he wanted a shed in someone's garden, and we would find one, but it would be in the wrong area or not the right garden. We made other attempts to fix his accommodation issues – caravans, even tool stores, knowing that he was not prepared to move into most housing situations. It was frequently exhausting. Finally, a defining moment occurred during one of our many lengthy late-night conversations, as we stood on the corner of Page Lane and George Street in the freezing cold.

He looked me in the eye, which was rare, and said, 'If I ever choose to give this up, it won't be on a night like this. It will be on warm summer's day.' This confirmed to me that this was a lifestyle he had chosen, and whatever anyone tried to do to help it was never going to be suitable in his opinion. As I relaxed into what would become a different dynamic for our friendship in the years that followed, I became convinced that he was on some kind of crusade, a mission to make a statement. I don't think I or anyone could fix Pete's 'homelessness' dilemma, because ultimately it was something he remained in control of. But I could choose to be a friend and we always had plenty to talk about.

An avid sportsman in the past, he loved watching sporting events screened on the big public TV in the square. He took particular delight in watching the rise of Mo Farah's athletic career, and avidly followed significant athletics championships. He was incredibly well read, deeply fascinated by literature; we and a few other people stored his ever-increasing collection of books. He wasn't so concerned about having somewhere dry for himself, but his books were another matter entirely. But it was conversation about music, preferably the music of the 1960s, that brought the most expression to his face and switched the light on in his eyes.

On one of those occasions, when he was waiting for me to finish talking to some Zac's Place regulars, he overheard our conversation and a disbelieving smile came across his face as he eavesdropped.

'What are you smiling at, Pete?' I asked curiously.

'For a moment there,' he said, 'I thought I heard you say Barry McGuire was going to be playing a gig at Zac's Place.'

'You did hear me say that, Pete. We've just fixed a date for the autumn.'

'What, *the* Barry McGuire, "Eve of Destruction" Barry McGuire?' he repeated, almost like an excited schoolboy.

'Yes, Pete, *the* Barry McGuire!'

He then reeled off all the lyrics, off the top of his head, to Barry's huge hit, 'Eve of Destruction'. He marvelled as I pulled up YouTube clips on my phone of old Barry McGuire footage and loved the ones where the Mamas and the Papas were Barry's backing band.

Knowing all the lyrics was typical of Pete, and it was a genuinely beautiful thing to see him fully alive in that moment. He could do the same for literature, reciting swathes of Shakespeare or Oscar Wilde, and long passages from the Bible. The Sermon on the Mount was a favourite, and his faith was searching and genuine. He would get very agitated when well-meaning people would place a gospel leaflet in his hand, assuming he needed converting, rather than engage him in conversation and discover that he was considerably closer to God than they might have thought. He followed closely the progress of his old school classmate Rowan Williams, on his journey to become Archbishop of Canterbury, a connection that would come back with greater poignancy several years later.

Pete became a one-man advertising hoarding for our gig with Barry McGuire. He insisted I print a large laminated weatherproof poster, which he would hold for hours on end in the city centre, day after day, in the lead-up to the gig. There he would stand, motionless, rain or shine, in the square, at intersections, at the entrance to the shops, holding the poster across his chest. The gig sold out and true to form Pete wouldn't come in, but we left the right doors and windows open for him to listen outside. He talked about that night until the day he died.

He didn't get to call it a day on a warm summer's evening, though. He died on a cold January morning from the effects of sepsis, an infection that could have been easily treated if he had been willing to accept help. The sparrows, feral cats and city rats had lost their breakfast partner and the warm morning sun would no longer rouse the pile of plastic sheets in Castle Square into eccentric life. On receiving the news of Pete's death from Jan, a nurse whose dedication to serving the homeless is a gift to the city, I wept.

The local media went into overdrive, devoting several pages every day to the story as people tried to piece together the mysterious life of Pete – only to discover that his name was actually Brian. I contacted Rowan Williams to share the news of Pete's death and give him some advance warning, knowing that the media would inevitably eventually make the connection between the two of them. They did, and sure enough it made the national press. In homage to Pete, or Brian as he was known at school, and showing Rowan's capacity to retain words, he was able to remember a short poem Pete had written in school around five decades previously. Simply entitled 'Crowds', it has an almost prophetic resonance:

> Crowds
> They are like sardines,
> Crushed, squashed in;
> But their cries are heard.

Rowan commented, 'I think he simply saw and experienced life from a different angle from the rest of us. He often had a smile on his face, but it was usually a smile that ever so slightly suggested that the joke was on everyone else.' I couldn't fix Pete's obvious problems, but maybe that wasn't what I was supposed to do; maybe I just needed to listen. Maybe, as it turns out, he was more fully alive than the rest of us.

I registered Pete's death, listing him not as of 'no fixed abode' but as residing at Castle Square, Swansea, because he was part of our community. A large number of people attended his funeral, and some weeks later I and another close friend placed his ashes in the unmarked grave of his mother, his stepfather and his brother in a simple, dignified ceremony. His death brought a huge outpouring of grief, and there were calls for a statue. The media ran with it for all it was worth. This disturbed me, though, because he would have been deeply uncomfortable with all that. As I wrestled with my own thoughts, the following was the response I made via my blog entry on 29 January 2015.

Is anyone listening?

A couple of winters ago I got a call from someone saying Pete was desperately down and needed some additional warm things. It was well below zero and the snow was falling onto packed ice. I put the snow chains on the van and headed into the city as quick as I could and true to form I found Pete, huddled up, peering out of his coat declaring that he was perfectly OK and had what he needed, wondering what all the fuss was about.

Pete was as complex as he was introverted, as intelligent as he was sober and as stubborn as he was opinionated. His stubborn refusal to engage with 'the system' infuriated me, and many others, only taking help if he believed it was truly benevolent, which to our community's credit was often in abundance. If, however, he thought anyone was receiving a salary for 'helping the homeless', they didn't meet the criteria to be in his circle of support, despite their efforts and care.

To get close to Pete was almost impossible. You had to earn that right and it wasn't anything to do with what you might offer of material gain or daily bread. There were no brief meaningful chats with Pete. You needed an hour at least before you even started.

A lyrical journey of sorting his predicament out, the struggles of a changing city around him, the ecstasy of watching Mo Farah win gold on 'his' wide screen TV in the square, reeling off Beach Boys and Mamas and Papas songs, the memories of being fit enough to play table tennis, the hypocrisy of government, society and the church and all the books he wanted to store, were all fair game, for any that were invited into the intimacy of a private audience with Pete.

What Pete wrestled with was the same as most of us, the reality that life is often about loss. The loss of innocence, of opportunity come and gone, of loved ones unexpectedly departing and the loss of love thought won.

People respond and react in many different ways. For Pete, he chose to try and lose Brian Burford in search of only he knew what and why. But for all the muddle and the riddles, he carried something in his soul, a crusade and mission to make a point maybe. He was not a statistic, or even a legend, he hated that thought, but he wanted to say 'something' on his terms and he wanted 'someone' to listen.

On occasion Pete would say, 'If I ever give this up, it won't be in the winter, it will be on a warm summer's day,' as if there could have been some far-off possibility that it could happen and he was in control of it.

We 'could' build a monument of bronze 100 feet high, or we could pause, we could watch, we could learn to listen. If we want to build a monument in memory of Pete, may it be one that taps into the core of our soul that compels us to love without measure or want of any reward, to leave our prejudice behind, to live simply and gather only what we need. May it be a monument of substance in the life of our community that levels the ground and doesn't place a person's worth on what we see with our eyes, but in the knowledge that we are all wonderfully made and indeed all very fragile.

Enjoy the dance, dear friend, the embrace, the banquet and the mansion. See you later, I'll be the one stood outside in the rain hoping you'll let me in.

Far greater than any statue, Pete's death fuelled an already established conversation in the city that has contributed further to a broader, more cohesive communal effort to support the most vulnerable people in Swansea. There are more volunteers and more community groups, more churches and other faith groups opening their doors, more free or subsidized community meals provided, more foodbanks, more donations to charities, more businesses taking social responsibility seriously and, most importantly, a greater awareness across the community of the complex needs of every individual on the margins of society. Occasionally there are still voices crying in the wilderness; best we keep our ears open.

15

Primary colours

There's something wonderful about witnessing a creative process take place before your eyes. None more so than seeing an oil painting come to life. Around the edge of the canvas the artist works the paint with the brushes, mixing, turning and smoothing to get the exact colour needed in every stroke, gradually adding a bit of this hue and that shade, until it's just right. Already there are shapes, colour and definition but the image is still flat, not fully alive yet. It's waiting for that spark of life.

In what seems like an age of mixing in the margins, in this creative process one solitary stroke is being formed. With the intuition only an artist has, the brush moves from the margins to the main body of the canvas. In this brief moment, a defining stroke of genius is added, bringing the whole canvas alive. It may be a broad stroke or the most delicate of touches that is so perfect that its influence goes way beyond the volume of paint transferred to the canvas.

Sometimes we see unexpected brush strokes of such clarity and definition amid those messy edges of our life experiences. For me, the edges have become a place of immense creativity and definition. It may look like a mismatched mix of colours that are not easy on the eye. The sunshine is mixed with the storms, but somewhere in the chaos are the rainbow strokes, light and shade alongside the laughter and the pain. Some defining marginal moments are spontaneous, some are unpredictable, unthinkable, unfathomable, others carefully crafted from just three primary colours. In the messy edges of what frames my life, the three primary colours of faith, hope and love have coloured, textured and defined the story. It is in the blending and working of those primary colours in our stories that I see the traces of the wider palette in gentleness, kindness, self-control, peace, joy, patience, goodness and faithfulness, all bringing the canvas alive in the brilliance of a spark of light in a dark place that invites us not to give up. I see the broad brush strokes of justice, of mercy and humility, creating a sunrise horizon that promises that things can be different; there is always the hope of a new dawn.

I see the colours of the Beatitudes of Jesus rooted in the faith that trusts in the grace that first reached out to receive those blessed kingdom gifts. I see their hues in the hope that while we may try and fail, and try and fail again, the colour shines in the attempt to live a different way now. I see their rainbow promises in how I choose to define and demonstrate love in a world that seeks it from a different kind of palette.

If I return again to the stream where I played as a child, I will still try and dam it up. There is always something of the child in everyone. Now older and wiser, though, I know that the stream has a source that will not suddenly stop and pay homage to my meagre engineering efforts. I know too that those waters have far greater journeys to make beyond my splashing around for a brief moment in time. There is an ocean that awaits way off downstream. As a child I was baptized in the waters, based on what I knew and accepted at the time. I have stayed living in those waters, explored the source of what lies upstream and look towards the ocean that awaits. The faith that trusts in the Father burns deeper still, the love of the Son keeps me cleansed in these waters, and the hope is in the comfort of the Holy Spirit that one day the canvas will be complete. But for now, I continue to search for the strokes of definition, for the threads of redemption, for the traces of those primary colours in all that I see.

In a progressively self-obsessed selfie culture, it would be easy to pull out the stories of how the great and the good have walked into my life and out again. As I have spent time recently reflecting on all the people I have met and what I have learned from them, the most consistent theme that arises has been realizing where those defining strokes of colour have occurred. It has not been in the company of the rich and the famous, or in the corridors of power, or among the popular in-crowd at the best parties. I have learned and matured most in the company of the misfits and outcasts, the poor and powerless, the sick and the dying, the abused and the hungry. Without a doubt, the weakest and most ostracized voices have had the most important things to teach me.

So where are things up to now? Zac's Place continues as a community of people, a church for ragamuffins, that finds its gathering point in Swansea city centre. It is still a place of complicated beauty and glorious chaos as the walking wounded work out what it means to follow Jesus. Discipleship is fostered in the service of the poor, alongside Bible teaching. As a venue, Zac's Place remains the last place in the city that even the most disruptive person will be banned from. As a community of people, it continues to be wholeheartedly committed in serving the poor, working in partnership with other churches and agencies in the city to do this. The voices of artists still resonate as our Beatitudes art commission moves out of our own space in order to tour in different venues.

Personally, I am working out what it is like to start and maintain something and then hand it all on. The track record of founders failing to hand over well is a well-worn path and one that I am wrestling with. The writing of this book runs parallel with my completion of a master's degree in Applied Theology which has an emphasis on developing leadership. I never expected to take the academic road, but it has proved to be fresh water for a weary soul and also a route to seeing a greater maturity of leadership develop and what I hope will be a venture that is sustainable in the longer term.

On a practical level, also while writing this book we have established a social enterprise to sustain the ongoing efforts at Zac's Place. Rough Edges was born in 2014 and is a charity shop with a male emphasis, a 'man cave' if you like, trading in donated items from sheds, workshops, gyms and gardens. It is staffed by an eclectic team of volunteers, some of whom have faced homelessness in the past while others have significant health issues and life stories that make it difficult to source other work, alongside retired people from a variety of skilled backgrounds. Rough Edges is showing great promise as a sustainable endeavour, and proving to be of genuine benefit to the staff and the wider community in its location in Townhill, Swansea.

God's Squad continues to develop in Europe and now has a history approaching 50 years in Australia. The biker subculture has faced challenges to its very existence in some countries and this will present a challenge to us too, I am sure. But God's Squad continues to be on the road, active in Christian ministry and service in many countries, and remains one of the most diverse lay ministries on the planet. Many chapters have members engaging in broader ministry among young people, among those trapped in addiction, in prisoner rehabilitation and in working for justice in a broken world. The healthiest God's Squad chapters always have an additional depth of ministry in addition to that within the bike scene. Having founded the club in the UK and previously served as both the first European President and International Vice President for quite some time, I remain active in the South Wales chapter, which is fully integrated into the life of Zac's Place. You will still find me on the road and in clubhouses seeking to influence the subculture with the love of Christ. I am still riding a matt black Harley; the current modified 1999 FXDX is fast approaching 100,000 miles and altogether I've covered somewhere in the region of

500,000 miles in the last 34 years. I will admit that these days I tend not ride sub-zero – the bones can't take it any more – unless it's for a funeral or the Reading Toy Run, which still rolls on over three decades later. The solitude of the bike remains a creative place for my mind and the open road is always a welcome invitation. The camaraderie of travelling with a bunch of mates still brings great satisfaction too, as I listen to the exhaust note of the guy in front, see his road-dirtied God's Squad colours, and catch sight of the grinning or grimacing (depending on the weather) of a club brother in my rear-view mirror knowing that he too has his own story to be thankful for.

Many of the people I have had the opportunity of sharing my life with are fragile and broken. A significant number struggle to get through each day, never mind from one month to the next or as far as the next birthday. For many, life is difficult most of the time, and that's why in the past they have resorted to chemical stimulants and patterns of behaviour that brought a swift fix, either to numb the pain or to feel good, or at least a bit better than the usual chaos.

I strongly believe that a real and present danger within the Evangelical Church in the West is that we have been sucked in to the temptation of fostering a feelings-based faith. We create performance environments and emotional highs that tug at the heartstrings and make people 'feel something'. I've been there, done it, survived it, and found it wanting. The danger with making people feel something first and foremost, and presenting this as the foundational platform for their faith, is that sooner or later their faith will be found wanting when encountering challenge, fear and doubt.

At the end of the Sermon on the Mount, Jesus alludes to this in the story of two builders (Matthew 7.24–29). One built his house on the beach, the other built further inland where the sub-base was more substantial and the foundations were solid. The wiser builder is likened to those who don't just hear the words of Jesus but put them into active service. There's a temptation, however, to believe that if we build on good foundations we have some kind of God-given immunity to the storms that come bowling in from the sea. Jesus' promise isn't immunity from the storms of life; his assurance is that a life built on following him is like having good foundations in the scariest and most damaging of storms. The windows may rattle and we may lose some roof tiles, but the structure stays strong. The foundations we build on are our choice. The bad times are a given – they will come to us all at some point. Life is hard, for some people unbelievably so, and grossly unfair.

Jesus encouraged a well-educated enquirer who asked the question, 'Of all the commandments, which is the most important?' (Mark 12.28–34), to love God with all his heart, all his soul, all his mind and all his strength and also love his neighbour as himself. There may be a tendency here to think that we are expected to come from a position of strength or superiority to begin with.

It's easy to imagine loving God with all my heart if I know that my heart is good, if it is full of a wealth of holiness, holding no malice. And there lies the problem. I know what my heart is like, and you know what your heart is like too, full of dark secrets. So how can we love God with all our heart? By the grace of God, we can know forgiveness, we can know cleansing, we can know what it's like to be accepted by God as holy. But to love God, with all of our heart? Is it really going to be acceptable to God when I'm too scared to look at it deeply myself, never mind allow God himself to see inside?

What if the very core of my soul can feel like a prison, even when I know the truth, even when I've tasted freedom? What about those times when my soul suffers as if my flesh has been gnawed away by vultures, exposing the nerve ends and bone? Can I really love God with all my soul, if my soul is a place of oppression and darkness?

What if the daily torment of mental health disorders t can wage war in our minds means that we need a concoction of pills just to function at the most basic level? What if the depressive laments of Jeremiah are my experience? What does loving God with all my mind look like then?

What if our strength has been sapped? What if we can't even muster the words to cry to God for help? Can we still love him if all we have left are the faintest breaths of life? Can we still find him if Job's exhausted affliction is our closest companion? Will he still be interested, or is he only interested in the pure ones, the beautiful ones, the together ones and the strong ones, those who look as if they have something to offer?

When Jesus advocates loving God with all our heart, soul, mind and strength, he knows exactly who he is talking to and can see the condition of our heart, the complexity of our soul, the clarity of our mind and our lack of strength. We start and continue this righteous road with Christ from where we are, not where we are not. This is a beautiful mystery to me.

The more I have sat in the gutter, listened to stories of heartbreak and pain, the more I have had to level with people and say, 'I'm sorry, I do not have an answer for you.' The more I have wrestled with my own darkness, the more I have discovered that the bruised, the broken and the battered can love God with a depth and sincerity that defies logic. All we can love God with is our all, in whatever state of repair or disrepair that is. There is no place for pretentious platitudes, cover-ups or a polished performance that hides the truth. Though we might wish otherwise, *we are not as strong as we think we are*, a sentiment that Rich Mullins captured beautifully in a song of the same name.

It becomes the most vulnerable place of faith, to stand as if naked, stripped bare. It's only then that we discover what our true colours are, as a defining stroke of genius from the creator's brush emerges from the margins of the canvas to reveal the kaleidoscope of colour and definition that places us in the image of Christ. Despite everything, we are loved, not betrayed. We are bruised, but not defeated. We discover the light of the world entering darkness, and as Rick Elias writes in his song 'Stripped', 'I am stripped but not afraid'.

Many years ago at a large biker gathering, I was talking to one of the organizers around the back of the site. It was an area used by the landowners as a dumping ground and there were piles of rubble with oil cans, car batteries, blown engines, tyres and other types of scrap. For the event it was the diesel store area for the generators, and it served as a quiet space for us to catch up and enjoy a drink together. As we were chatting, he stopped and tilted the brim of his hat towards the mountain of junk, pointing to a solitary wild flower, a poppy defiantly standing tall and beautiful in a polluted wasteland. In a previous conversation in a smoky clubhouse he had told me that his favourite Bible story was that of the widow's mite (Mark 12.41–44), which comes just a few sentences after the story of the man who asked about the most important commandment. A man who has lived life to a number of excesses and paid a price for them was captivated by both a solitary flower and a story of a vulnerable widow. It was a precious image. The kingdom of heaven is made of these moments.

Jesus was in the temple with his friends. A number of wealthy people were putting stacks of money in the collection pots and making a bit of a performance about it. Does that sound familiar? Then he points out a poor widow to his companions. She comes and places two small coins, worth just a fraction of a penny, into the receptacle, unnoticed by the popular wealthy donors who appear, in their own eyes at least, to have a hotline to God. But Jesus, for whom no detail of the heart went unnoticed, commends her actions, pointing out to his followers that in comparison she has given more than anyone in that temple. She has in fact given everything, all that she had, no matter how insignificant, no matter how fragile. She had given her all because that's all she had. This anecdote has nothing to do with money, but everything to do with the giving of ourselves in obedience and in response to the grace and mercy of God's love.

When I consider so many of my friends, my travelling companions and those at Zac's Place, I have to ask: how can we give all when we have nothing left to give? How can we love God with all our heart when it's busted and broken? Or our soul when it's dark and tested? Or our mind when it's blown and confused? Or our strength when it's sapped? I think we do it with an honest appraisal of where we are at, and we begin at the place where Jesus encouraged his friends to begin: poverty of spirit.

Many years ago I chose the road I wanted to take. The road with Christ has indeed been a wild ride at times, but it's been a road that breathes life, even in the face of death. It's a road I could leave at any point and occasionally it can seem like an attractive option to bail out. It has exhausted me, strung me out and driven me to points of utter despair at times, but the words of the only man ever to have walked this earth and come out of the whole human experience alive continue to convince me and enthuse me to pursue the righteous life, with a righteousness that surpasses that of the Pharisees and the scribes. It is a righteousness that is not bound up in my ability to perform well, it is the gift of a poppy in the wasteland, it is the gift of a Saviour washing road-dirtied feet.

Acknowledgements

The majority of this book was written between 2013 and 2017 at the Society of the Sacred Heart in Llannerchwen in Brecon, South Wales and Mucknell Abbey, in Worcestershire, England. Latter stages were completed at Llangasty Retreat House, Nicholaston House and St Madoc Centre, all in South Wales. I am deeply appreciative of the hospitality, welcome and ministry of the brothers and sisters at each of these communities.

My thanks to each person who has encouraged me to 'write these stories down', especially to Martin Hughes. Thank you also to those who have given me permission to use part of their own story, or their loved one's story, as part of mine. Some names have been changed or excluded altogether for confidentiality, and some of the language in the dialogue I have toned down as I think some readers would have found the original offensive, but neither detract from the truth of the stories.

I am grateful to Tony Collins for seeing the potential and the whole team at SPCK for their enthusiastic commitment to this project. Thanks are also due to John Corcoran, Chris Jack, Janet Keauffling, Raymond Sauter, Arfon Jones and my family, who have been vital sounding boards in my search for integrity in my writing.

My life has been enriched by an eclectic mix of travelling companions along the way: friends, encouragers, supporters, influencers and shapers. Some have been around for a lifetime, others briefly at pivotal moments of significant influence. Many are still around; some have made the departure to the great dance before me. My deepest thanks therefore to: James Stewart, Stephen Spicer, David and Grace Turner, Steve and Alison Gorman, Jan and Andrew Manley, Abby and Ruth Hanson,

Alan and Marjorie McCarley, Joanie Yoder, Barry and Bunny Kirk, Paul and Wendy Elford, Ann and John Lawley, Ken and Christine Wiltshire, John and Val Smith, the TFC community, Ben and Jane Spiller, Derek Toome, Paul Mills, Roy Crowne, Martyn Joseph, John and Glena Smith, Sammy Horner, Stuart Burns, Eugene and Jan Peterson, Dave Cave, Alistair Hornal, Bryan Roberts, Rowan Williams, Lorraine King, Liz Hinds, Ron Willoughby, Glenn and Ros Stewart, Norman Ivison, Karen Carter, Ian Coffey, Jeremy Steeds, and all those who have faithfully supported this ministry over the past three decades.

My deepest thanks to the beautiful community of people who have made up the Zac's Place family, and to your resilience, and your faith. Our shared experience is quite wonderful in its brokenness. The dedicated and caring volunteers who are and have been part of the Zac's Place coffee bar and breakfast crews are diamonds, as are those who lead the Tribal Gatherings alongside me, those who keep the venue running and the Rough Edges crew – thank you all. The vast array of musicians who have played under the Zac's Place banner at our own venue, in bars, on festival stages, in prisons and on television are too many to list, but our lives have been richer for your gift. Along with our Beatitudes artists, may the influence of your art continue to inspire.

The original CMA Reading branch and the wider UK membership of those early days was foundational and I remain grateful for those years and all the friendships that have continued. The Reading Toy Run crew are proof that friendships formed in the freezing cold are some of the best you will have. My thanks to those who have worked on my bikes and kept me on the road amid laughter, friendship and much head shaking, especially, Grub, Yorkie and the Wills.

To the international community of God's Squad CMC, present and past, and our families, my love and thanks; especially fellow UK founders Howie, Dave, Spike, Psycho and

Soldier, in addition to Smithy and the Melbourne chapter circa 1995. I remain dumbfounded by God's grace and count it an honour to have shared this road with you. Similarly Ducky, Magoo, Billabong, Wes, Buckshot and Isak, who together have weathered the trials of international leadership alongside me beyond the call of duty – my utmost respect and appreciation of your companionship. My immense gratitude to my own GSCMC South Wales chapter who keep me grounded, and especially to Ric, who has kept so many wheels turning, often in my absence.

My deepest thanks also to all my friends in motorcycle clubs who have welcomed me and my club brothers into your club-houses, your homes and your lives. Thank you for giving us the space to do what we do.

Grace and peace,
Sean Stillman, Swansea

All the author's royalties from the sales of this book are being donated to Exousia Trust, a registered charity in Great Britain, No. 1002581.

For more information, feedback or contact, visit <www. zacsplace.org> or write to: Exousia Trust, Zac's Place, George Street, Swansea SA1 4HH, UK.

Notes

1 Copyright © 2007 Stewart Henderson. Used with the author's permission. Not to be reproduced in any form, whatsoever, without prior agreement with the author. 'Meek Abundance' was commissioned by Sean Stillman for the Zac's Place Beatitudes collection.
2 Bethany Barnett, *About Face: Finding Peace Within the Battle*, Dublin: The Joy Bee, 2017.
3 John Chrysostom, *On Living Simply*, ed. Robert Van De Weyer, Liguori, MO: Liguori Publications, 1997, p. 52.
4 Sean Stillman, 'These Colours', 2007.
5 'A Zac's Place Lament', 2016, edited by Liz Hinds.

Further reading

I offer this list as a guide to publications that have offered helpful insight around some of the subjects I have written about, that have a personal connection to my own story, and sources I have referenced.

Barnett, Bethany, *About Face: Finding Peace Within the Battle*. Dublin: The Joy Bee, 2017.

Cain, Susan, *Quiet: The Power of Introverts in a World That Can't Stop Talking*. London: Penguin, 2013.

Chrysostom, John, *On Living Simply: The Golden Voice of Saint John Chrysostom*, ed. Robert Van De Weyer. Liguori, MO: Liguori Publications, 1997.

France, R. T., *The Gospel of Matthew*. Grand Rapids, MI: Eerdmans, 2007.

Hauerwas, Stanley, *Matthew*. London: SCM Press, 2006.

Henderson, Stewart, *A Poet's Notebook . . . with new poems, obviously*. Oxford: Lion Hudson, 2018.

King, Martin Luther, 'Love Your Enemies', *Journal of Religious Thought*, 27, no. 2, 1970, 31–41.

Manning, Brennan, *The Ragamuffin Gospel*. Colorado Springs, CO: Multnomah, 2005.

Moxen, David, *Tarore and the Spread of the Gospel*. NZCMS, 2014. <www.nzcms.org.nz/200-years/2014-pilgrimage/2014-tarore/> retrieved 20 November 2017.

Smith, John, *Cutting Edge*. Tunbridge Wells: Monarch, 1992.

Smith, John and Doney, Malcolm, *On the Side of the Angels*. Oxford: Lion, 1987.

Snyder, Howard A., *The Radical Wesley: The Patterns and Practices of a Movement Maker*. Franklin, TN: Seedbed, 1996.

Stott, John, *The Message of the Sermon on the Mount*. Leicester: IVP, 1978.

Vardy, P. and Grosch, P., *The Puzzle of Ethics*. London: Fount, 1994.

Wright, Tom, *Virtue Reborn*. London: SPCK, 2010.

Photograph acknowledgements

Is anyone listening? Occasionally there are still voices crying in the wilderness, 'Pete': Lee Aspland

Blessed are those who mourn, for they will be comforted. The captivating life-size sculpture, affectionately called 'Doris', who is part of the Zac's Place Beatitudes commission: sculpture by Steve Spicer, photograph by Sean Stillman

On the road with fellow God's Squad CMC South Wales member, Martin, 2010: Wes Bungay

In full flight at Swansea Grand theatre at a fundraising gig, 2016: Linda Wellington, LW Photography

All other images: Sean Stillman